Studien zur Neuen Politischen Ökonomie

Herausgegeben von
T. Bräuninger, Mannheim, Deutschland
M. Bussmann, Greifswald, Deutschland
G. Schneider, Konstanz, Deutschland

Martin Brunner

Parliaments and Legislative Activity

Motivations for Bill Introduction

Springer VS

Martin Brunner
Konstanz, Germany

Zugl. Dissertation der Universität Konstanz,
Erstgutachter: Professor Thomas Bräuninger,
Zweitgutachter: Professor Gerald Schneider,
Tag der mündlichen Prüfung: 06.02.2012

ISBN 978-3-531-19611-4 ISBN 978-3-531-19612-1 (eBook)
DOI 10.1007/978-3-531-19612-1

The Deutsche Nationalbibliothek lists this publication in the Deutsche Nationalbibliografie; detailed bibliographic data are available in the Internet at http://dnb.d-nb.de.

Library of Congress Control Number: 2012950145

Springer VS

Printed on acid-free paper

Springer VS is a brand of Springer DE. Springer DE is part of Springer Science+Business Media.
www.springer-vs.de

Contents

Acknowledgements

to write is to travel
Michel Butor 1974

Writing this book often felt like a long journey toward some yet unknown destination. Many hours of this journey were literal travel: For three years, the Deutsche Bahn has been a reliable means of transportation between Konstanz, where I live, and Mannheim, where I work.

The journey of my writing most of the time resembled more an alpine climb than travelling by train. I would not have mangaged the climb without knowledgeable guides. My deep thanks go to my advisor, Prof. Thomas Bräuninger, who put his trust in me, supported me on the rough patches, and generously shared his experience. Not a guide to lead on well-trodden paths, he always encouraged me to explore my own trails. I am also grateful to Prof. Gerald Schneider, who agreed to act as second examiner, as well as to Prof. Susumu Shikano for chairing my thesis defense committee.

Co-travelers were great companions along the way. I am very grateful for feedback, advice, and other support from my colleagues and friends. Special thanks go to Marc Debus and to Thomas Däubler – who both undertook some smaller "detours" with me as co-authors – as well as to fellow doctoral students and postdocs in Konstanz and Mannheim – in particular, Julian Bernauer, Nathalie Giger, Susanne Michalik, and Jochen Müller for their input in colloquia and for their moral support. I also wish to thank the various generations of research assistants in Konstanz and Mannheim, who have contributed to the preparation of the data set used in this study. Finally, I thank the DFG for funding the Emmy Noether group "Comparative Legislation", led by Thomas Bräuninger, in which I participated.

Having a secure base camp where to retreat and replenish one's resources is an indispensable precondition for a safe expedition. I thank my friends, especially Christian Schudy and Florian Kunze, who have given me good moments away from my desk and laptop. My deep gratitude goes to my parents for their love and support over the years. Finally, I thank Julia, who has read through all versions of this book. I am happy that we will be travel companions for more and other journeys to come.

Mannheim, August 2012
Martin Brunner

1 Introduction: The Puzzle of Parliamentary Bill Introduction

In a democratic system that is drafted according to the classic separation of powers ideal, the tasks of political institutions are easily identified: The legislature makes laws, the executive executes laws, and the judiciary interprets the law and solves disputes. In modern parliamentary democracies parties play a central role in parliamentary elections as well as in government formation. Through party government, the agenda-setting power nowadays lies mainly with the government (Döring 1995a, 1995b). As a consequence, the old dualism of parliament and government has been replaced by a new dualism of government and opposition. "Making and breaking governments" (Laver 2006: 122) has superseded legislation as the most important task of parliament. The task of law production has shifted toward government: Most laws in modern parliamentary democracies originate from government initiatives. Olson and Norton (1996: 7) even formulate a 90 percent rule – a catchy phrase to describe the dominance of government in the legislative process and the declining role of parliaments in legislation in Western European democracies: "In most cases, the 90 per cent rule applies, with 90 per cent of legislative activity being initiated by the executive, which gets 90 per cent of what it wants".

The weak role of parliament in the legislative process is a dominant view in the literature. Yet, the 90 percent rule is oversimplifying matters, and at least the first part of the rule ("90 per cent of legislative activity being initiated by the executive") is empirically wrong for most parliamentary democracies. Even though parliaments have mostly only kept a law-influencing instead of a law-making power, parliamentarians still make considerable use of their right to initiate legislation. However, the success rates of these parliamentary initiatives are low in most systems. This constitutes an empirical puzzle. This puzzle is even more pronounced for the opposition, which is usually more active and less successful than the parliamentary majority. The question arises then: Why do parties or individual MPs introduce so many bills even though these legislative initiatives almost never get adopted and their chance to influence policy outcomes is almost nil?

With this study of parliamentary bill introduction I aim to contribute to solving this puzzle and thereby fill a research gap. Due to the fact that policy outcomes are mainly shaped by governments and their parliamentary majorities in parliamentary democracies, literature on parliamentary decision-making focuses mainly on institutional and partisan factors influencing policy outcomes. Policy preferences of the political actors as well as their bargaining strength due to institutional conditions are among the most prominent factors studied to explain outcomes (e.g. Laver and Shepsle 1996, Tsebelis 2002). In research focusing on legislative output opposition parties are usually neglected. Opposition parties have a place in the analyses only in contexts when institutional conditions assure the influence of parties that do not participate in government. This can be the case when there are different party majorities in the two chambers in bicameral systems (Tsebelis and Money 1997), or when government parties have to enter temporary coalitions with opposition parties in parliament in the case of minority governments (Strøm 1990), or in the case of supermajorities needed to pass legislation (e.g. the two-third majority requirement in Germany to change the constitution).

The research presented here takes a different perspective on legislation: Instead of looking at the output and the processes leading to those specific results, as most research does, this study sheds light on the input in parliament. Whereas opposition parties and government backbenchers usually have very limited influence on the content of the laws actually adopted, they are very active in proposing legislation. One explanation, of course, could be that opposition parties and backbenchers have a lot of stamina and try again and again to find a parliamentary majority for their proposals. In this case one would expect rather technical bills or bills that represent compromise positions in order to find majorities. The low probability of getting bills adopted could also encourage alternative strategies in bill introduction. I argue that instead of influencing policies directly, opposition bills (as well as bills proposed by backbenchers of the parliamentary majority[1]) mainly serve different purposes: Bills are used in order to signal own policy positions and to show alternatives to government policies. Or they point at topics that rank high on the public agenda but low on the government agenda. They can also be a means for individual MPs to build up an independent personal profile. If bills are used this way, they serve as a vote-seeking rather than a policy-seeking tool.

1 In the theoretical discussions as well as in the analyses, I focus on cases where government coalitions and legislative coalitions are identical. Therefore, if not otherwise specified, I only refer to government parties and not to opposition parties when speaking of the parliamentary majority.

In this study I will focus on the vote-seeking motivation of introducing bills. Chapter 2 introduces a formal model of oppositional bill introduction on the party level, which shows that sponsoring bills is consistent with the assumption of vote-seeking parties that want to signal their policy positions. Comparative empirical evidence from Belgium, France, Germany, and the United Kingdom is provided. Chapter 3 focuses on the use of bills and other parliamentary activities to respond to public opinion. Working with empirical evidence from the German Bundestag, the chapter analyzes whether and how parliamentary activities are responsive to public opinion, whether there are differences between the responsiveness of opposition, government, and parliamentary majority, and in how far upcoming elections influence responsiveness to public opinion. Chapter 4 adopts an individual level perspective and examines the motivation of individual MPs to use bill sponsorship in order to distance themselves from their party and to build up a personal vote. The theoretical model is tested with data from the French Assemblée Nationale.

The major contributions of this study are the following: It develops consistent formal models for the party and the individual level and tests the model implications empirically, it shifts the focus away from policy output to policy input and to the motivation of opposition, which is often neglected in research. Finally, it shows the fruitfulness of adopting an individual level perspective in research on bill sponsorship in parliamentary democracies.

In the remainder of this introductory chapter, I will present the puzzle of oppositional and backbench bill introduction in more detail on the basis of comparative data. I will then give a short review of the literature on legislation and opposition and discuss evidence for oppositional bills as policy-seeking tools. Subsequently, I will demonstrate, with a short case study, that it is plausible to assume that bills serve vote-seeking purposes. Finally, I present my research strategy in greater detail and give an extended overview of the subsequent chapters of this study.

1.1 Parliamentary Bills in Comparative Perspective

The dominance of government in all stages of legislation is often claimed in the literature but hardly ever backed up with data. Especially rare is comparative data on the bill introduction behavior of opposition parties. Even though the new dualism suggests that it is important to focus on the differences between government (including parliamentary majority) and opposition, research often only reports aggregate data on legislative activities of government and of parliament as a whole. The Inter-Parliamentary Union (IPU) (1986) provides data on bill introduction between 1978 and 1982 for a large sample of 83 countries. However, this data has a number of shortcomings. Tsebelis (1995: 95-6) states the descriptive statistics of the IPU as follows: "In more than 50 percent of all countries, governments introduce more than 90 percent of the bills. Moreover, the probability of success of these bills is very high: over 60 percent of bills pass with probability greater than .9, and over 85 percent of bills pass with probability greater than .8 (Inter-Parliamentary Union 1986: Table 29 [sic!])."[2]

Even though Tsebelis (1995) writes about law production in parliamentary democracies, the IPU data contains also information on authoritarian states. This fact drives the dominance of governments found in this data. Especially in the socialist countries contained in the sample, government had a monopoly regarding the introduction of legislation. Consequently, the summary statistics provided by the IPU are not very helpful in the context of parliamentary democracies.[3] If one regards only democratic states, the picture of governments' dominance becomes more nuanced: Andeweg and Nijzink (1995: 171) present evidence for 15 European parliamentary democracies based on the IPU data with corrections made for Belgium and the Netherlands.[4] The information in Table 1 is based on their corrected data.

In the 15 Western European parliamentary democracies the success rate of government bills is still very high (with a median of 93 percent, and only Belgium, Portugal, and Greece with a success rate below 80 percent). However, there is also a significant number of parliamentary initiatives. The claim that over 90 percent of bills are introduced by government only holds in three cases – Luxemburg, the Netherlands, and Norway. On average, more than 30 percent of the bills have their origin in parliament. In four countries (Belgium, France, the United Kingdom, and Sweden), parliamentary bills even exceed the number of government bills. The success rate of parliamentary bills reaches from zero percent in Greece to 57 percent in Germany. The data shows that parliamentary initiatives make up a substantial proportion of legislative activities, which should not simply be neglected in analyses. The large difference between the success rates of bills with a parliamentary origin indicate that they serve a different function in different countries. Unfortunately, the data does not distinguish between

2 The data to which Tsebelis refers is actually not in Table 29 but in Table 31 (Inter-Parliamentary Union 1986: 910-11).

3 As a politically neutral international organization the IPU does not distinguish between legislation in democratic and authoritarian states. Overlooking this fact about the IPU data might also be the source of the misleading 90 percent rule mentioned above.

4 Döring (1995a: 594, footnote 2) reports even more flaws of the IPU data. In addition to the country experts on Belgium and the Netherlands, the experts on Sweden in Döring (1995c) also find that the data reported by the IPU does not match the official national statistics.

parliamentary bills introduced by opposition and parliamentary bills introduced by the government parties. One would expect that due to the close relationship between government and parliamentary majority, the success rates as well as the incentives to introduce bills should differ between parliamentary opposition and parliamentary majority.

Table 1 Average Number of Bills Introduced and Passed per Year in the Lower House of 15 Western European Democracies (1978-1982)

	Government		Parliament	
	Introduced	Passed	Introduced	Passed
Austria	74	71	40	20
Belgium	55	29	187	11
Denmark	171	151	89	5
Finland	259	253	238	3
France	93	77	328	11
Germany	79	80	28	16
Greece	128	98	19	0
Luxemburg	63	64	4	1
Netherlands	135	119	6	2
Norway	75	74	8	1
Portugal	126	17	55	26
Spain	80	65	57	8
Sweden	± 200	most	± 2400	± 1%
Switzerland	± 80	most	11	1
United Kingdom	57	53	100	10

Source: Andeweg and Nijzink (1995: 171)

Data allowing for such a distinction is difficult to obtain. An edited volume on legislation in Western Europe (Ismayr 2008a) with country chapters on the 15 "old" member states of the European Union gives respective data only for Germany, Luxemburg, and Spain. The other country chapters distinguish between government bills and parliamentary bills in their overview tables on the number of bills introduced and their success rates, but fail to provide information on bill introduced by opposition.[5] Nevertheless, I report the information for all countries as the data covers a longer time period than the dated IPU data. The overall picture as presented in Table 2 confirms what could already be seen in the IPU data. The first part of the 90 percent rule only applies to a minority of countries. In the Netherlands, for instance, government almost holds a monopoly on bill introduction. Likewise, in Luxemburg and Greece legislative input is clearly dominated by government. However, in eight of the 14 countries presented in the table the picture is reversed: In these countries the number of parliamentary bills exceeds the number of government bills introduced. The second part of the 90 percent rule applies in most Western European parliamentary democracies. In most cases government bills get adopted. Only in Italy and Portugal government success rates are below 80 percent.

In general, parliamentary bills are much less likely to succeed. Only in Belgium, Italy, Portugal, and Germany more than ten percent of the parliamentary bills are successful. When distinguishing between government and opposition bills two interesting patterns become apparent: Opposition parties introduce considerably more bills than the parliamentary majority (at least in the three countries for which more detailed data on parliamentary bills is available). Their success rate, however, is much lower (between 0.6 percent in Germany and 5.1 percent in Spain). The success rate of bills introduced by MPs or parties belonging to the parliamentary majority reaches much higher levels (between 20 percent in Luxemburg and 70.5 percent in Germany). Hence, the puzzle of parliamentary bill introduction is even more puzzling for opposition bills.

5 For Sweden and the Netherlands no information on the success rate was available. For Austria aggregate information on the number of bills introduced and passed is missing altogether.

Table 2 Average Number of Bills Introduced per Year and Success Rates in Western European Democracies

	Government Bills	Parliamentary Bills		Period
Belgium	143* (91.1%)	246 (10.2%)		1991-2003
Denmark	246 (93.1%)	39 (7.7%)		1992-2000
Finland	239 (83%)	369 (1.4%)		1945-2002
France	91 (89.4%)	241 (6.7%)		1958-2002
Greece	106 (87.7%)	14 (2.3%)		1977-2004
Ireland	51 (86.9%)	14 (2.6%)		1997-2004
Italy	300 (77.9%)	773** (17.4%)		1948-1996
Netherlands	248 (-)	8 (-)		1999-2003
Portugal	47 (71.2%)	168 (33.5%)		1976-2005
Sweden	115 (-)	1897 (-)		1960-2004
UK	38 (95.6%)	92 (8.2%)		1995-2004
		Parl. Majority	Opposition	
Germany	96 (87.5%)	24 (70.5%)	38 (0.6%)	1983-2005
Luxemburg	95 (90%)	4 (20%)	10 (1.9%)	1995-2005
Spain	40 (88.8%)	4 (38.4%)	51 (5.1%)	1986-2004

Note: The numbers reported are yearly averages over the period stated in the last column. The success rates of government and parliamentary bills are given in parentheses.

* Government bills and Senate bills that were adopted in Senate.

** This number encompasses Senate bills that were adopted in Senate. These bills amount to approximately seven percent of the total number of bills. These bills might bias the success rate of parliamentary bills upwards.

Sources: My own calculations based on the country chapters in Ismayr (2008a). The information in these chapters is mostly based on official sources and calculations of the authors. *Finland*: Wiberg (2004, cited in Auffermann/Laakso 2008: 77), *Sweden*: Jann/Tiessen (2008: 115), *Denmark*: Nannestadt (2008: 137), *UK*: Saalfeld (2008a: 168), *Ireland*: Saalfeld (2008b: 207), *France*: Kimmel (2008: 244-5), *Netherlands*: Timmermans et al. (2008: 279), *Belgium*: Woydt (2008: 327), *Luxemburg*: Schroen (2008: 360), *Germany*: Ismayr (2008b: 391, 404), *Italy*: Weber (2008: 479, 482), *Spain*:

Santaolalla (2008: 522), *Portugal*: Claro da Fonseca/Guerra Martins (2008: 570), *Greece*: Zervakis/Chanos (2008: 630). The relevant data for *Austria* is not reported in Pelinka (2008).

The difficulties for the authors of the country chapters in Ismayr (2008a) to distinguish between parliamentary majority and opposition bills are associated with the different rules that regulate parliamentary bills in different countries. In Germany, for example, bill introduction is a collective right. Individual bill sponsorship is excluded by the condition that a bill can only be introduced by at least five percent of the Members of Parliament or (as is usually the case) by an entire parliamentary party group.[6] Distinguishing between opposition bills and parliamentary majority bills can be easily done in Germany, as the party group bills are signed in the name of the entire party group. The official statistics also present aggregate information on the bills sponsored by the different party groups.[7] In a comparative perspective, the numerical restrictions are the most severe in Germany, but there are also some other Western European countries, namely Austria, Italy, and Spain, which demand more than one MP to introduce a bill (Mattson 1995: 458). In Spain, at least 15 MPs are needed in order to introduce a legislative proposal; however, in practice, parliamentary initiatives are introduced by entire party groups (Santaolalla 2008: 527).

In most other countries bill introduction is an individual right. In Belgium, Luxemburg, and Portugal, even upper limits for the number of initiators exist in an attempt to avoid binding too many MPs before the examination of the bill (Mattson 1995: 457). In these countries, the partisan aspect of bill initiation is often of minor importance as many MPs rather pursue individual or constituency instead of partisan goals with their bills. This individuality is often also reflected in the actual written legislative proposal, which the initiators only sign with their name, without giving their party affiliation (this is the case, for example, in Austria, France, and the United Kingdom).[8] Thus, the official parliamentary statistics

6 However, when the Green party failed to reach the five percent threshold in West Germany in 1990, and only eight party members in the East entered the Bundestag, these MPs were nevertheless granted basically equal rights as an official party group (*Fraktion*). The same is true for the PDS in 1994, when they received only 4.4 percent of the overall votes, but entered Bundestag with 30 members thanks to four direct mandates (Saalfeld 2000b).

7 Compare http://www.bundestag.de/dokumente/parlamentsdokumentation/index.html, accessed on 26 October 2011.

8 In Germany, on the contrary, government parties often disguise the individual authorship of bills: Many government party bills are not signed individually. This is especially true for bills that were handed out by the government. For *Gruppenanträge* (bills that do not find the support of a party group but of individual MPs) and bills sponsored by opposition party groups it is possible to identify the sponsors and co-sponsors of a bill. In Belgium, where bill introduction is an indi-

in these countries often do not associate the bills with parliamentary majority or opposition but simply present aggregate numbers of private members' bills. Consequently, it is more difficult to get information on the patterns of oppositional bill sponsorship in these countries.

For the project "Comparative Legislation"[9] detailed information on individual bills has been collected for four countries: Belgium, France, Germany, and the United Kingdom. This detailed data allows distinguishing between government, parliamentary majority, and parliamentary opposition activities as well as joint parliamentary activities of government and opposition parties. This information is reported in Table 3.

Table 3 Bill Introduction in Belgium, France, Germany, and the United Kingdom

	Government	Government Parties	Mixed Initiatives	Opposition Initiatives	Total
Belgium	1015 (91.0%)	1766 (10.3%)	329 (37.1%)	2139 (3.0%)	5249 (24.6%)
France	714 (67.6%)	1867 (5.7%)	5 (20.0%)	2150 (0.7%)	4736 (12.8%)
Germany	1573* (90.2%)	426 (79.6%)	110 (84.6%)	658 (2.0%)	2767 (67.3%)
UK	371 (94.1%)	675 (13.2%)	16 (93.8%)	778 (4.2%)	1840 (26.4%)

Note: Total number of bills introduced in the first chamber (Belgium 1988-2003, France 1986-2002, Germany 1987-2002, UK 1987-2003); percentage of successful bills in parentheses.

* In Germany, government bills are first sent to the *Bundesrat* (the second chamber) before they are introduced in the Bundestag. In order to give an impression of the success rate of government bills, information on these bills is included in this table. For the other countries only the government bills introduced in the first chamber are shown. However, the success rates of government bills introduced in the first and the second chamber reach similar levels.

vidual right, but where parties are strong, authors of bills sign with their name and their party affiliation.

9 Project leader: Thomas Bräuninger, Deutsche Forschungsgemeinschaft (DFG) project number BR 1851/3. For details on data sources and coding of the data, compare Brunner and Debus (2006).

The right to introduce legislation is used extensively by parliamentarians of opposition as well as of government parties. The numbers of bills introduced differ dramatically between the countries as shown in Table 3. Most bills are introduced in Belgium and France, where MPs meet the fewest restrictions, whereas in Germany and the United Kingdom, with their more restrictive rules, the overall numbers of bills are much lower.[10] In all countries but Germany, the number of parliamentary bills by opposition as well as by the majority parties exceeds the number of government bills.[11] While the success rate for opposition bills is low in all countries (between less than one percent in France and four percent in the United Kingdom – or in numbers: between 13 in Germany and 64 in Belgium), the chance of adoption for bills initiated by government parties varies largely: Whereas in France only six percent of all private members' bills initiated by government MPs get adopted, in Germany 80 percent of the government parties' bills are successful. The high German success rate is easily explained as bills by parliamentary majority parties are almost always supported by all party groups of the coalition partners, and hence already have the support of the majority in the Bundestag at their introduction. Given the strong party discipline, adoption is very likely.[12]

Overall, the reported findings point to some difficulties in comparing bill introduction in different settings. Formal rules, such as the numerical restrictions of a high minimal number of initiators in Germany or the very restrictive rules of

---

10 For Germany, it has already been mentioned that bill introduction is a collective right. In the United Kingdom, four different procedures with very different restrictions for the introduction of private members' bills in the House of Commons exist: the Ballot Rule, the Ten Minute Rule, Ordinary Presentation, and taking up private members' bills introduced in the House of Lords. For the latter three rules there are severe time constraints. For Ballot Rule bills more time is available. However, as the name already suggests, it is a gamble whether an MP gets the change to introduce a bill this way: At the beginning of each parliamentary session, there is a lottery held in which usually more than 400 MPs participate. 20 MPs are drawn from the ballot and have the right to introduce their bills in the order in which they are drawn. The little time available for dealing with private members' bills is first of all used for these bills. The first ten MPs can even claim some refunds for their expenses in drafting the bill. As not all MPs participating in the ballot have a clear idea which bill they would like to introduce, colleagues, pressure groups, or also government often try to hand out bills to them.

11 Even if one considers all government bills in these countries (that is, also the bills that are first introduced in the second chamber) parliamentary bills still account for more than two-third of the total number of bills. Overall 1688 government bills were introduced in Belgium, 1444 in France, and 519 in the United Kingdom. The overall success rates were 93.1 percent, 67.9 percent, and 95.0 percent, respectively.

12 In Germany, the restriction to introduce bills jointly or in mutual agreement is sometimes even part of the coalition agreement (Däubler 2011). Similarly, Belgian government party MPs are bound to a certain degree by the coalition agreements (de Winter and Dumont 2003).

introduction in the United Kingdom, can account for different levels of bill initiation. The electoral systems provide MPs with different incentives for rather seeking a personal vote or a party vote (Carey and Shugart 1995). These differences can also be reflected in the bill sponsorship behavior (Bräuninger et al. 2012). Differences in political culture can likewise account for the number and content of bills sponsored. In Belgium, for example, the formal rules leave a large leeway to individual legislative activities. In practice, however, partisan influence often seems to prevail, as MPs have to ask permission by their parties and depend on party-based research assistance (de Winter and Dumont 2006). Finally, also the meanings of "law" differ over the countries (Trantas 1995).

Differences in the rights, procedure, political culture, the domain of law, and electoral incentives can account for some of the differences observed between countries. But it is remarkable that, notwithstanding the very different institutional setups, very similar patterns of oppositional (and to some extent backbench) bill introduction can be observed. After reviewing the state of research, I will try to contribute to solving this puzzle in this study. Are oppositional and backbench bills just "much ado about nothing"? Or can systematic patterns be found that explain rationally the time and effort put into seemingly hopeless attempts to change policy?

1.2 Parliamentary Bills between Neglect, Party, and Policy

Studies on legislative politics in parliamentary democracies usually claim the dominant role of government, observe the "decline of parliaments", and focus on the policy outputs. The declining power of parliament is seen as a consequence of factors such as the growing importance of professional, disciplined parties and the increasing complexity of policy-making, which have strengthened the influence of government. The influence of international bodies such as the European Union or of organized interests outside of parliament are also frequently mentioned as factors undermining parliamentary power (compare e.g. Norton 1988 for an overview). In line with the assumption of the declining role of parliaments, studies concerned with policy outcomes frequently see a direct link between the party composition of government and policy outcomes, while neglecting parliamentary influence or institutional constraints (e.g. Hibbs 1977).

The formation and termination of government coalitions is therefore often at the center of attention of studies dealing with parliamentary democracies (Riker 1962, Axelrod 1970, Austen-Smith and Banks 1988, Lupia and Strøm 1995, Laver and Shepsle 1996, Laver and Schofield 1998). These studies also often think of parties as unitary actors that seek policy and office gains, they most of the time maintain that governments are sovereign, and some even assume ministerial discretion with direct influence on policy outcomes. More recent research highlights that parliaments still play an important role through parliamentary oversight (Saalfeld 2000a) but also in the formulation of policies: Martin and Vanberg (2004, 2005, 2011) emphasize the importance of legislative institutions to control ministers in coalition governments and to enforce coalition compromise. Especially strong committees are found to play an essential role in this respect. Also with respect to duration and success of government bills, the division between coalition partners or also between government and opposition has been identified as particularly important (Martin 2004, Becker and Saalfeld 2004, Bräuninger et al. 2008).

In some cases oppositional influence on policy output is also analyzed. Oppositional influence plays a role, for instance, in situations with different party majorities in bicameral systems (Tsebelis and Money 1997, Manow and Burkhart 2007), or, in the case of minority governments, when legislative coalitions differ from executive coalitions in membership (Strøm 1990: 69). Schmidt (1996) argues that partisan influence on public policy can be expected especially in majoritarian systems. When political and institutional circumstances allow for co-governance of opposition, the potential that partisan differences lead to distinct policy outcomes is limited. Oppositional influence on policy outcomes can be expected foremost in consensus democracies (Lijphart 1999). Helms (2004) characterizes Germany as a prototype of a parliament-centered opposition with strong veto and co-governing powers for minority parties.

Even though this research brings parliaments and the phase between government formation and termination into focus, incentives for the introduction of parliamentary bills and especially opposition bills are still neglected. However, when one takes a closer look at legislation in parliamentary democracies, one can observe, as discussed above, that notwithstanding their low success rates a considerable amount of bills stem from within parliament across (almost) all parliamentary systems. Particularly the parties in opposition make use of legislative initiatives, even though their proposals are rarely adopted. One important reason for the low success rate of oppositional initiatives is what Cox (2006) describes as the "legislative bottleneck": Legislatures have time constraints and therefore cannot discuss all legislative proposals. Government control of the agenda solves this problem but leads to the exclusion of the opposition from the legislative process (compare also Mattson 1995 for different forms of restrictions for private members' bill introduction). Mostly unable to influence policy directly opposition has to find ways to deal with its exclusion from the legislative agenda.

Cook (1989: 130) identifies three strategic choices for minority leaders in the US Congress to react to their restricted role in agenda-setting. First, they can work behind the scenes, trying to find compromises on the issues to be taken up. Second, they can go public with alternatives to issues put on the agenda by the majority parties. Third, they can put issues on the public agenda which they think have been neglected by the majority. Whereas Cook focuses on the connection between media and legislation, I concentrate exclusively on the legislative side. Nevertheless, I argue that bills introduced in parliament also reflect the strategic choices mentioned by Cook. Either the bills seek compromise and have the goal of eventually being taken up by government, or they represent alternatives to government proposals, or they emphasize issues that government has not (yet) put on the agenda. When leaving the perspective of (opposition) party leaders, bills could also serve a fourth strategic choice: Individual parliamentarians could use bills to signal their own agenda in order to win a personal vote or to promote their career.

Literature on the reasons for bill sponsorship is quite rare. There are some articles that examine the sources of (co-)sponsorship in the United States and that follow a similar path as I do (e.g. Campbell 1982, Herrick and Moore 1993, Schiller 1995, Garand and Burke 2006). In the context of European democracies such studies are even rarer. Mattson (1995) analyzes the conditions for private members' initiatives in comparative perspective. While he focuses on the possibilities of bill introduction and their chances to be successful, he neglects the incentives for sponsoring bills. One exception is a recent article by Bowler (2010), who looks for an electoral connection in the sponsorship of private members' bills in the United Kingdom. Other fruitful starting points are literatures on pork barrel politics (e.g. Lancester and Patterson 1990, Stratmann and Baur 2002), responsiveness (e.g. Miller and Stokes 1963, Page et al. 1984, Brettschneider 1995, Hobolt and Klemmensen 2008), or the personal vote (e.g. Mayhew 1974, Cain et al. 1987, Norton and Wood 1993). Similarly, the analysis of another kind of legislative behavior, namely roll-call votes, could be helpful to get to the roots of what drives politicians decisions' in this context. Again, most of these studies focus on the Anglo-Saxon context and on the output of bills. In the subsequent Chapters 2 through 4 the relevant literature for the specific research questions will be reviewed in more detail.

Policy-seeking Aspects in Parliamentary Bills

In the chapters that follow, I will focus on the choices of using oppositional bills as instruments to signal the opposition parties' own position as alternatives to government policies, to emphasize topics that the public cares about, or to serve as a tool to gain a personal vote. All these aspects of oppositional bill sponsorship have in common that oppositional bills (and private members' bills) are primarily seen as a vote-seeking tool. The first choice mentioned above (working behind the scenes and reaching compromise) does not have a large vote-winning potential. Instead, policy-seeking aspects prevail in this case. In general, while the sheer number of unsuccessful opposition and backbench bills suggests that policy-seeking is not the major explanatory factor for the introduction of such bills, it cannot be excluded categorically. In the following, I will present some evidence for policy-seeking aspects in these bills. The focus of the study in the subsequent chapters, however, will be primarily on vote-seeking motivations, which I assume to be the dominant explanation for the majority of opposition and backbencher bills.

Yet, in some contexts it is likely that policy-seeking motivations prevail, especially when bills are introduced by leading figures of government parties or entire party groups or, as usually the case in Germany, jointly by all government party groups. Such bills are often prepared in the ministries and then handed out to parliamentarians or party groups (compare Rudzio 2006: 225-30 for Germany, Duhamel and Parodi 1988: 549 for France, or House of Commons 2010b for the United Kingdom). The reasons for such disguised government or "handout" bills usually lie in the institutional setup. In Belgium or in France, government has to get the opinion of the Council of State (*Conseil d'État*) before introducing bills in parliament. Handing out such bills can be a means of saving time. The same is true for Germany, where government has to get the opinion of the Bundesrat in a first step. Introducing a duplicate of the government bill as a party group bill in Bundestag can save time. Such bills that have the support of government are usually successful.

This does not apply for opposition or backbencher bills. A closer look at the 13 opposition bills that were adopted in the German Bundestag between 1987 and 2002 reveals that only a few were indeed successful in shaping policy in exactly the way the opposition bill had intended. Just in two cases opposition bills were the only source of the policy proposal and were adopted without further changes. However, the issues dealt with were of rather minor importance, uncontroversial and only affected a small group of people: One bill was concerned with the discrimination of blind people in the code of criminal procedure (printed paper of the Bundestag DRS 11/816) and the second bill addressed the ratification of the International Covenant on Civil and Political Rights (DRS 12/556). The other eleven successful opposition bills were either identical with propositions by the parliamentary majority[13] or the bills were substantially modi-

13 DRS 11/6317, DRS 12/1630, DRS 12/3609, DRS 12/4532, DRS 14/2904.

fied in the committees,[14] so that in some cases the opposition even voted against their own proposal in the end.[15]

While direct policy influence of opposition bills is a rather implausible incentive for bill introduction in most cases, Sebaldt (1992) suggests an indirect influence of oppositional legislative activities, which could be a source of inspiration of government legislation. In his study Sebaldt analyzes which of the bills adopted in Germany between 1949 and 1987 can be traced back to opposition initiatives. Overall, he finds evidence that around eleven percent of all bills (excluding ratification laws) have their origin in opposition initiatives (Sebaldt 1992: 160). When looking at the data in more detail, this record becomes less impressive, however. The majority of these bills are only of marginal importance, and most have influenced government activities only indirectly. More importantly, oppositional influence is declining over time. While 32 opposition bills were directly successful in the first legislative period of the Bundestag, only eight bills were successful if we take the ninth and tenth legislative period together. The indirect influence also declines over time (Sebaldt 1992: 205). The more recent data I presented above suggests a further decline at least in directly successful opposition bills: As little as 13 bills were successful in the legislative periods 11 through 14. While directly after the Second World War inexperienced government, newly constructed ministries, and a high need for new laws and regulations created a good environment for policy influence of opposition, the need and possibilities for oppositional policy influence have declined over time.

Certainly, some of the parliamentary bills are indeed serious attempts to change policy directly. This is unquestionably true for bills handed out by government in order to save time or to disguise the authorship for other reasons, but also for some opposition bills that target mainly smaller technical issues. Nevertheless, policy motivations are not a satisfying explanation for the major part of oppositional and backbench legislative initiatives. In the subsequent Chapters 2 through 4, I will concentrate on other explanatory factors, which put vote-seeking motivations at the center of attention.

---

14 DRS 12/2560, DRS 12/2975, DRS 13/27, DRS 13/1736, 13/3594, DRS 13/7864.

15 The discussion of successful oppositional private members' bills in France in Chapter 4 reveals the same picture.

1.3 A Look behind the Scenes: The Coffee Tax

The amount to which policy-seeking motivations or strategic vote-seeking considerations prevail in the actors' motivations to start parliamentary activities is not easily observable. The approach followed in the subsequent chapters of this study, in order to derive information on the motivations of political actors, is to model the strategic incentives of these actors and to analyze available process data of actual parliamentary activities. Interviewing political actors would be a different approach to exploring the motivations that drive opposition and backbench MPs to introduce bills even though the chance of influencing policy this way is low. The shortcomings of such an approach would be that the interviewees are likely to give socially desirable answers instead of revealing actual strategic considerations. The little case study that follows on the legislative activities around the "coffee tax" in Germany in the early 1950s and 60s of the 20th century uses another source for some insights from behind the scenes: Minutes of the cabinet meetings reveal interesting aspects concerning the government's point of view on the role of opposition and parliamentary majority in legislation.

Such information can be accessed on the website of the German Federal archive,[16] which offers minutes of cabinet meetings of the federal government between 1949 and 1965 under the Christian Democratic chancellors Adenauer (1949-1963) and Erhard (1963-1966). In these minutes several aspects on the interactions between government, parliamentary majority, and parliamentary opposition in Germany can be seen. For instance, in a cabinet meeting one minister insists that more time is needed before his colleague should introduce his bill: He deems it necessary to first overcome the differences between the coalition partners, as it would be a very awkward situation for government if the parliamentary opposition would support the bill whereas the parliamentary majority criticizes it.[17] In another meeting Chancellor Adenauer proposes to write letters to the party group leaders of the coalition partners in which to insist "emphatically" that they should support the legislative program of the government during the legislative period.[18] Likewise, evidence for pressure on MPs of the parliamentary majority not to pursue certain legislative initiatives[19] as well as for handing out bills to the parliamentary majority[20] can be found. Opposition bills are often mentioned as factors that put time pressure on government. For instance, ministers mention the need to quickly introduce a government bill in response to ru-

16 http://www.bundesarchiv.de/cocoon/barch/0000/k/index.html, accessed on 3 November 2011.

17 58th cabinet meeting, 13 April 1950, agenda item 8.

18 76th cabinet meeting, 15 May 1963, agenda item 2.

19 Compare, for instance, 73rd cabinet meeting, 24 April 1963, agenda item 7.

20 152nd cabinet meeting, 19 September 1956, agenda item 12.

mors that opposition is preparing a bill on the same topic, or a bill has to be introduced at once, as an opposition bill on the topic will enter the committee phase soon.[21] Evidence for electoral considerations can be found as well, such as Chancellor Adenauer's request to hurry the preparation of a certain bill in order to get it adopted before the "electoral fever" starts[22], or Adenauer's warning that the upcoming Bundestag elections will be lost if the problem of the pension reform will not be solved in a timely and generous manner.[23]

In the following, I will present the discussions on the reduction of the "coffee tax" in some more detail, as it combines a number of different aspects of bill introduction that can be found in these minutes of cabinet meetings. On 1 October 1952, the Bundestag voted with a large majority for a motion for leave introduced by MPs of all parties in order to ask the minister of finance to introduce a bill on tax reductions for coffee and tea. The Bundesrat agreed on the reductions for tea but was against reductions for coffee, fearing large tax falls. On 17 November 1952, the drafts for such tax reductions were presented in the cabinet[24] meeting as part of the draft budget law for 1953. A positive decision was taken by the cabinet ten days later. However, in January 1953, the minister of finance, Schäffer (CSU; 1949-1957), voiced his opposition against tax reductions for coffee and tea due to the expected tax falls. The majority in cabinet continued to support tax cuts. State Secretary Lenz (CDU) of the Bundeskanzleramt (Federal Chancellery) formulated his support the most directly. He claimed that large parts of the population had even stronger feelings about the coffee tax reductions than about the intended income tax reductions. With a view to the upcoming elections, Lenz insisted that something should be done that is generally welcomed by the voters and especially appreciated by housewives.[25]

In March 1953, Chancellor Adenauer informed his cabinet that he had been notified that the oppositional SPD prepared the introduction of a bill to reduce the coffee tax from ten German marks to three German marks per kilogram coffee. Adenauer and the majority of the cabinet agreed that under these circumstances a majority for tax cuts could hardly be avoided in the Bundestag. The introduction of an alternative government proposal was rejected by the minister of finance, who insisted that, given the financial situation, he could not take the

---

21 Compare, for instance, 15th cabinet meeting, 3 August 1953, agenda item 1; 171st cabinet meeting, 15 February 1957, agenda item 2; 20th cabinet meeting, 21 March 1962, agenda item B; 75th cabinet meeting, 7 May 1963, agenda item B.

22 84th cabinet meeting, 2 June 1955, agenda item E.

23 157th cabinet meeting, 17 October 1956, agenda item 4.

24 The government coalition in power from 1949 to 1953 consisted of the following parties: CDU/CSU, FDP, and DP.

25 269th cabinet meeting, 16 January 1953, agenda item 8.

responsibility for a government bill leading to tax falls. Before the SPD initiative was even introduced in April 1953, the government's parliamentary majority also prepared an initiative to reduce the coffee tax, however, after the intervention of the minister of finance, this bills was stopped.[26]

In a special meeting in May 1953, during which the federal government debated the topic with coalition MPs, the MPs claimed ("in a very extensive discussion") that a majority in favor of the coffee tax reductions could hardly be avoided. Several MPs also pointed out the likely electoral relevance of the issue: If the reductions were rejected, the psychological effects on the general public, especially on the female electorate, would be immense. The coffee tax reductions should thus be treated with a higher priority than other bills that might be of a higher objective relevance. Chancellor Adenauer, however, insisted that the authority of the minister of finance was not to be undermined. The acceptance of the coffee tax reductions would bring the minister in a difficult situation. Therefore a compromise between the interests of the Bundestag and the ministry of finance needed to be found.[27]

In June 1953, the minister of finance introduced a bill that was supposed to lead to 20 percent tax reductions on coffee. The bill received the support of the cabinet but went against the vote of the minister of economic affairs, Erhard (CDU; 1949-1963), who still insisted on a reduction to three German marks, as proposed by the opposition.[28] In a special meeting of the federal government, one day before the committee of finance of the Bundestag was to deal with the government and opposition proposals on the coffee tax reduction, the minister of finance tried to close the ranks in cabinet. The minister of economic affairs declared that he had given strict order that nobody representing his ministry would comment on the government proposal in the committee. However, if questioned by the committee on the economic facts and developments, he would answer to the best of his knowledge. And as the calculations and estimations of the ministry of finance were wrong, he would not defend them in public. Furthermore, he formulated the expectation that the committee would reject the government proposal and accept the opposition bill. He argued that, also for political reasons, the government should not oppose the committee's decision. The Vice-Chancellor, Blücher (FDP; 1949-1957), stated his general agreement with the minister of economic affairs but insisted that the cabinet had to stand behind its former decision to introduce the government proposal. The Chancellor likewise insisted to stay with the decision, to wait and see what the Bundestag would do, and to

---

26 285th cabinet meeting, 31 March 1953, agenda item 5.

27 Special meeting of the federal government, 20 May 1953, agenda item 1.

28 296th cabinet meeting, 2 June 1953, agenda item 5.

solve the disputes between the ministries.[29] One day later, the finance and tax committee rejected the government bill with a large majority and agreed with an even larger majority on supporting the opposition bill. The bill was adopted in the Bundestag and published on 30 July 1953 (Federal Law Gazette I 708).[30]

The coffee tax reductions saw an interesting aftermath. In 1959, when the CDU/CSU governed without coalition partners, the coffee tax was increased again. In 1960, the minister of finance, Etzel (CDU; 1957-1961), informed his colleagues about the motions of the opposition to reduce the coffee tax and about similar tendencies among the coalition partners. He asked for and received the permission to inform the coalition parties that the government would take all measures in line with the constitution to prevent cuts in revenues.[31] Afterwards, several initiatives of the SPD to reduce the tax were rejected.[32] But there was also international pressure on the German government to reduce the coffee tax. After the 1961 Bundestag elections, when the CDU/CSU formed a coalition with the FDP, the minister of economic affairs urged his colleagues to reduce the tax. He warned that at the upcoming GATT (general agreement on tariffs and trade) meeting, Germany would be put in the dock for the fifth time for the highest taxation of coffee in international comparison. The new minister of finance, Starke (FDP; 1961-1962), however, insisted that he could not accept the loss of several hundred million German marks of internal revenue.[33] The next time this issue was on the cabinet agenda, the minister of finance insisted that cabinet find a common position against coffee tax reductions, especially since the FDP had agreed with the SPD in the past on the need for further tax reductions. The minister of economic affairs on the other hand reported that the need for coffee tax reductions had been on the agenda of his personal conversation with President Kennedy of the United States.[34] Notwithstanding national and international pressure, the next coffee tax reductions were not realized until 1968 by the first Grand Coalition of CDU/CSU and SPD.[35] The coffee tax lasts until today. Germany still has the highest coffee tax rate among the few countries in the European Union that raise a coffee tax (Kuck 2011).

---

29 Special meeting of the federal government, 16 June 1953, agenda item 5.

30 Compare footnote 13 on the minutes of the special meeting of the federal government, 16 June 1953, agenda item 5.

31 100th cabinet meeting, 16 March 1960, agenda item G.

32 2nd cabinet meeting, 23 November 1961, agenda item C.

33 3rd cabinet meeting, 27 November 1961, agenda item B.

34 7th cabinet meeting, 22 January 1962, agenda item C.

35 "Zweites Gesetz zur Änderung des Kaffeesteuergesetzes", 17 December 1968 (Federal Law Gazette I 1334).

The example of the coffee tax allows interesting insights in a number of aspects concerning bill introduction. It can be observed that the minister of finance has the power to delay or even prevent policy proposals that his colleagues or the parliamentary majority would like to realize for political reasons. Internal division along party lines and between resorts as well as financial restrictions and international pressures are among the factors that can influence and delay cabinet decision-making. In the relationship between government and its parliamentary majority, the different incentives of MPs and government become apparent: Whereas especially the minister of finance needs to have the larger picture in mind, MPs seem more tempted to look for electoral rewards. The power of government to stop unwelcome initiatives of the parliamentary majority could be seen, as well as the limitations of government influence on the voting behavior, especially when the cabinet is divided. The oppositional strategy to put a popular topic on the agenda shortly before elections forced the government to become active. In the coffee tax case, due to the division within government and between government and the parliamentary majority, the SPD even managed to have a bill with large financial implications adopted. After the elections, however, the minister of finance succeeded in closing the ranks again and in defending the remains of the coffee tax against all internal and external pressures.

Certainly, the analysis of the cabinet minutes cannot give a complete picture of parliamentary bill introduction. Parliamentary bills that are discussed in cabinet meetings are likely to be a biased sample of all parliamentary bills. Bills will only make it on the cabinet agenda if they raise important issues, interfere with government projects, or bare the potential of dividing the cabinet or the coalition partners, or if they have a large vote-winning potential. Government might not care about bills that are only directed toward some geographic constituency or that intend to mobilize party supporters. It is also questionable whether such a policy success as described in the coffee tax would still be possible today when parties are more professional. Nevertheless, the above look behind the scenes shows the importance of electoral considerations and public opinion in the strategic interactions of the central actors as well as the close connections between government and parliamentary majority, at least in the case of Germany. In the subsequent chapters, I will generate further insights in patterns of bill introduction from a larger sample of cases.

1.4 Research Strategy and Plan of the Book

The information on parliamentary bills presented so far suggests a reformulation of the puzzle of parliamentary bill introduction. Policy motivation can account for bills initiated by government parties in the German Bundestag and also for joint initiatives by government and opposition parties (so-called mixed initiatives). Also in the United Kingdom, and to a lesser degree in Belgium and France, mixed initiatives get frequently adopted. And whereas government party bills have a much lower success rate than in Germany in those countries, they are still more often successful than opposition bills.

The puzzle of why bills are introduced that are unlikely to succeed consequently applies foremost for opposition and backbencher bills. The focus of this study will be on finding theoretical explanations and empirical evidence for the motivation for introducing such bills.[36] The theoretical models as well as the empirical parts will concentrate on bill introduction in the first chamber of parliament. Members of second chambers usually also have the right to introduce bills, but differences between the roles of second chambers in the respective political systems make it difficult not only to compare motivations for introducing legislation between second chambers of countries but also between members of first and second chambers within countries.[37] Analyzing the motivations for bill introduction in second chambers is therefore beyond the scope of this study.

---

36 The question of why parliamentary parties do not leave bill introduction to government alone, which has much more resources for the preparation of bills, is not dealt with here. Incentives for government to hand out bills to government parties or government MPs have already been mentioned above. A more detailed discussion of reasons for government party bill introduction can be found in Däubler's (2011) analysis of bills by the parliamentary majority in the German Bundestag. On the same token one could ask why government and opposition cooperate to introduce mixed bills. One explanation could be supermajority requirements. A more detailed analysis of such mixed initiatives can be found in Bräuninger and Debus (2010).

37 Before the revisions of the Belgian constitution in 1993 Belgium was an example of strong bicameralism with virtually equal rights for both chambers (Lijphart 1999). In this case, bill introduction in the Belgian Senate could be expected to have been based on similar motivations as in the first chamber. The federal reforms, however, changed the composition and influence of the Senate dramatically and actually transformed it into a "*chambre de reflexion*" (Depré and Renders 1996). Some of the senators are elected directly by the Flemish and the French electoral college, some are appointed by the community councils and others are "co-opted" by the other senators. In addition, the children of the King are senators by right. Belgian senators do not get a wage for their work and they have less staff than the members of the first chamber (Woyke 1999: 370). In the case of France, the powers of the Senate in legislation are limited to delaying the adoption of bills. Senators are elected indirectly by an electoral college composed of 150,000 so-called "grands électeurs". Due to the composition of the electoral college, which over-represents electors from the rural areas, the Senate had a conservative majority until the most recent Senate

The research presented here belongs to the field of comparative politics. I follow an empirical-analytical approach in solving the puzzle of seemingly wasted efforts in bill introduction by opposition parties and MPs as well as government backbenchers that can be observed in a wide range of political systems. The research strategy to solve this puzzle is influenced by the EITM (Empirical Implications of Theoretical Models) approach (Aldrich et al. 2008). I develop coherent formal models from which I derive hypotheses that are then tested empirically. In line with the divide identified above between the importance of partisan influence and activities on the one hand and incentives for individual legislative behavior on the other hand, I develop two separate game theoretic models, one to identify incentives for bill introduction on the party level, and another to explain patterns of bill introduction on the individual level.

The hypotheses on opposition parties' and backbenchers' motivations for drafting bills, derived from theoretical models of bill introduction, are tested using statistical methods to analyze empirical data. The basis for the statistical analyses in the subsequent chapters is a unique data set comprising information on all bills[38] introduced in Germany, Belgium, France, and the United Kingdom

elections in 2011. During the period studied here, senators were elected for nine years, one third of them being reelected every three years. In Germany, the Bundesrat has a very strong position in legislation for as long as state interests are concerned. In the Bundesrat, the governments of the German Länder are represented. Their voting weights depend on the population size of the state, but small states receive an over-proportional weight. The votes of a single state cannot be split. For an analysis of Bundesrat bills, compare Brunner and Debus (2008) and Bräuninger et al. (2010). Finally, the United Kingdom has the weakest second chamber of all countries selected for this study. The only power the House of Lords holds, is to delay legislation. Yet, Tsebelis and Money (1997) show that this power can be enough to influence policy outcomes. However, the Salisbury Doctrine states that the opposition with a majority in the House of Lords does not delay government initiatives that are based on electoral campaign promises and hence already have the majority of the voters supporting them. Therefore the House of Lords can be seen as a mainly deliberative chamber. Its weak position originates from its weak democratic foundation. Until the House of Lords reform act in 1999 most members were hereditary peers. Even though today only few hereditary peers rest in the House of Lords, its members are still appointed for life. Consequently, they do not have the pressure to get reelected, neither by any constituency, nor by parties.

38 As information on all bills is covered, the data represents an entire population rather than a sample. Still, as I want to go beyond pure description and make inferences about causal effects and report the uncertainty of conclusions (King et al. 1994: 9), I apply methods of inferential statistics to analyze the data. According to Broscheid and Gschwend (2005: O-23), this approach is more conservative than to simply interpret substantial effects of coefficients without considering measures of uncertainty. Taking the uncertainty of the estimates into account can be justified as the empirical tests of hypotheses are subject to a number of stochastic processes, even for data that is not the product of random sampling. These "errors" can stem from measurement errors in the dependent variable, a non-deterministic data-generation process, and the fact that every mod-

between 1986 and 2003[39] as well as information on institutional and partisan characteristics. As already mentioned above, the data set was constructed for the project "Comparative Legislation". The selection of the countries follows a "most different systems" approach (Przeworski and Teune 1970) concerning the institutional structure and legislative procedures. In the following chapter, which introduces a formal model of bill introduction as a means of signaling parties' policy positions, information on all four countries will be used for an empirical test of the model. However, I analyze bill introduction patterns separately for the respective countries, as major differences in the rules and procedures make cross-country comparison problematic. Focusing on the within-country variance allows to hold most institutional and cultural factors constant. Since comparable data is not available for all countries studied, Chapters 3 and 4 each concentrate on one country respectively. The data used here offers new possibilities to analyze the patterns of bill introduction in the selected countries. This is of special interest as reasons other than changing policies have rarely been studied in past research. Hence, the present study has the potential to widen our understanding of bill introduction.

The three subsequent chapters approach the puzzle of oppositional and backbench bill introduction from different perspectives:

Chapter 2: Parliamentary Bills as Party Policy Signals

In Chapter 2, parliamentary bill introduction is analyzed on the party level. As the classical view on parliamentary democracies with their strong and disciplined parties suggests, parties are the central actors in shaping political competition and policy-making in these systems and are therefore the right starting point to look for motivations of bill introduction. In this chapter, I adopt the view of the new dualism between government and opposition; consequently, government backbencher bills are neglected for the time being. I argue that instead of seeking policy, opposition parties use bill sponsorship as a means to signal policy positions out of vote-seeking motivations. The argument is formalized via the con-

---

el is a simplification of the true process and therefore likely to suffer from omitted variable bias (Broscheid and Gschwend 2005). Behnke (2005) advances a more restrictive view on the use of methods of inference statistics in the study of entire populations. For more on this topic from the frequentist and Baysian perspective, including a discussion of "super populations", compare Berk et al. (1995a, 1995b), Bollen (1995), Firebaugh (1995), and Rubin (1995).

39 The data set covers at least four legislative periods for all four countries. For some countries, also information on a longer time period is available: Belgium 1988-2007, France 1986-2002, Germany 1976-2002, United Kingdom 1987-2003. For Chapter 3, the German data has been extended until 2005.

struction of a game theoretic model. The empirical implications of the model are then tested with the data described above on bill introduction in Belgium, France, Germany, and the United Kingdom. The empirical results suggest that at least some of the factors expected to matter indeed influence patterns of parliamentary bill introduction. Governments as well as parliamentary parties introduce fewer bills on policy dimensions on which they hold positions that are expected to have a lower vote-winning potential. Furthermore, higher costs of bill introduction lower the expected number of bills introduced. Interestingly, some differences between Germany and the other three countries can be observed in the patterns of bill introduction. Whereas the party level seems to be the right level to analyze bill introduction in Germany, individual patterns of bill introduction in the other countries are overlooked by the approach adopted in Chapter 2.

Chapter 3: Public Opinion and Parliamentary Activities

Before shifting the analysis to the individual level, another aspect of bill introduction, and more broadly of parliamentary activities, is examined in Chapter 3 in more detail and again at the party level. Party programs and election manifestos can serve as an important source for drafting bills that transport policy signals. However, these programs are rather static and inflexible. Parliamentary activities could also be used to react in a more flexible manner to new problems or to shifts in the public perception of the importance of certain problems. In this chapter, I examine whether bills are responsive to shifts in public opinion. The focus is rather on responsiveness to the salience of issues than to positions of the public. Three questions are to be answered in this chapter: Is there responsiveness of political actors to the public perception of the most urgent political problems? Does the status of being in government or in opposition influence the responsiveness of parliamentary activities? Does the closeness of elections have an influence on the responsiveness to public concerns? For the empirical investigation of these problems, data on parliamentary activities of the different actors in the German Bundestag and on the "most important problems", as perceived by the public, are used. As expected, opposition parties are able to react more flexibly to public opinion, but also some evidence for the influence of the closeness of elections can be found.

Chapter 4: Private Members' Bills between Party and Constituency

When, unlike in Germany, individual bill sponsorship is possible, party factors are probably not the only and possibly not even the most important factors influencing bill introduction. In Chapter 4, I develop a formal model of bill introduction that systematically takes partisan and constituency pressures into account that influence the decisions of individual MPs. The empirical implications of the model are then tested with data from the French Assemblée Nationale. The French electoral system provides MPs with vast opportunities to sponsor low-cost bills, combined with strong incentives for MPs to seek a personal vote in their constituency. The results show that in addition to cost factors constituency demands as well as party factors are important in shaping MPs' bill sponsorship behavior. However, the analyses in this chapter also demonstrate that it is important to distinguish between bills according to their authorship. In particular, bills introduced individually follow the mechanisms described in the model and can serve to signal deviation from the party line and to generate a personal vote. For co-authored bills the pattern is less clear. In addition, there are also bills supported by entire party groups whose motivations are better explained on the partisan level.

2 Parliamentary Bills as Party Policy Signals

This study aims at solving the puzzle of why opposition parties and government backbenchers in parliamentary democracies introduce a considerable amount of bills even though these bills are almost never adopted. As discussed in the preceding chapter, previous explanations of bill introduction from the floor in parliamentary systems are theoretically underdeveloped and lack systematic empirical analysis of the motivations for bill introduction. The policy effects of such "policy proposals" are limited, as a closer look at the successfully adopted opposition bills has shown: They are usually only of minor importance and mainly bureaucratic in nature, or they undergo considerable amendments by the parliamentary majority before adoption. Consequently, the goal of influencing policy output directly, which is usually connected with bill introduction, can be excluded as a rational explanation for most parts of oppositional bill sponsorship. In terms of direct policy influence, these bills would be a waste of resources. The same is true for a large proportion of private members' bills irrespective of the government status of their sponsors, as in most parliamentary democracies private members' bills have a comparatively low success rate for MPs from government parties as well as for MPs from opposition parties. An individual level perspective of private members' bill introduction will be taken in Chapter 4 of this study. In the present chapter, I will focus on party level explanations.

Instead of influencing policy directly, parliamentary bills might also be directed at the general public and might be the result of primarily vote-seeking rather than policy-seeking considerations. Winning votes in the next elections could be a first step toward gaining office and finally realizing the party's policy agenda. In order to win votes, bills could serve as policy signals toward the voters. In this chapter, I develop a formal model of bill introduction in order to show that the introduction of oppositional bills can be explained rationally when one considers factors other than changing policy. I show that vote-seeking incentives can motivate an opposition party to use bill introduction as a signal of its policy position. The incentives of the parliamentary majority are not explicitly modeled here. Concerning bills handed out to the parliamentary majority by government, the incentives for bill introduction should resemble those of government. Concerning private members' bills, or bills introduced by government parties individually, it can be assumed that these bills have similar functions as oppositional bills.

The chapter is structured as follows: I will first review models of legislation and identify the difficulties of applying these models to the context of oppositional bill introduction in parliamentary democracies. Then I present a newly developed formal model of bill introduction as a simultaneous move game in which government and opposition decide strategically whether or not to signal their position on an issue by introducing a bill. Following the formal model, I give empirical evidence for the hypotheses derived. The final section of this chapter provides a conclusion.

2.1 Models of Legislation in Parliamentary Democracies

Oppositional bill introduction, and to some extent also more broadly parliamentary bill introduction, is a puzzle hardly dealt with in the literature. When opposition bills or private members' bills are discussed, the focus is often on formal rules instead of explanation (Mattson 1995), or the authors offer only ad hoc explanations, which are not really tested (compare, e.g., the various country chapters in Ismayr 2008a). In the conclusion to a special issue on comparing and classifying legislatures, Arter (2006: 466) makes the "broad observation" that "a significant proportion of private members' bills may be introduced with no serious intention of formulating and enacting new legislation or influencing government legislation. They are principally a means of profiling the legislator and/or his (usually opposition-based) party". A systematic treatment of incentives to introduce such bills is mostly missing in the context of European parliamentary democracies.[40]

For the United States Congress, where executive bills are formally forbidden, a number of models of the legislative process have been developed. McCormick and Tollison (1981) model the demand for and supply of legislation in terms of an interest-group theory of government. Politicians are seen as brokers who establish an equilibrium on the market of legislation. Yet, opposition or backbenchers without the power to actually provide legislation do not play a role in this model. Likewise, Baron and Ferejohn (1989) have elaborated an influential model on bargaining in legislatures. However, their model does not lend itself to an application to the question of oppositional activities in parliamentary democracies since it fails to include disciplined parties and because the role of

[40] Exceptions are Bräuninger and Debus (2010) who analyze bipartisan bills, and Däubler (2011) who investigates reasons for parliamentary bill introduction of governing parties. A systematic analysis of opposition bills, however, is still missing.

the executive in legislation differs crucially. Neither do other approaches in the study of legislative activities in the US Congress offer substantial help for the questions to be answered here. For instance, the literature on gridlock and divided government (e.g. Krehbiel 1998, Alesina and Rosenthal 1995) is deeply rooted in the US context. The same is true for other approaches in the legislative studies literature, which focus, for example, on institutional specificities such as the committee structure (Shepsle and Weingast 1981). Many of these studies have inspired research also outside of the United States context, even though such models are often difficult to transfer. For my purposes, it is not the institutional context, but the concentration on the explanation of gridlock or specific policy outcomes rather than on policy input that makes them unsuitable.

The institutional differences between presidential and parliamentary systems often make the transfer of legislative models from one system to the other problematic. However, also between parliamentary systems there are large differences in the institutional setup and hence in the legislative game that political actors face. Several authors in the US context deal with the question of motivations for bill introduction from an individual level perspective. These approaches will be discussed in Chapter 4. Whereas such approaches are of little predictive power for a political system of, say, Germany with its restrictive rules on legislation, they can still help discover the incentives behind the introduction of private members' bills in other parliamentary democracies.

The models discussed above have in common that they assume that policy goals are attempted and can be reached, or at least that policy output can be influenced. The presidential system with its lack of disciplining measures of the executive on the legislature and vice versa, such as the dissolution of parliament or the vote of no confidence, provides a substantially different institutional setup than parliamentary democracies. In parliamentary democracies with disciplined majorities direct oppositional influence on policies is usually not the case. Here, it is only under "exceptional" circumstances that the opposition can influence policy goals directly (minority government, supermajority requirements for changes of the constitution, or majorities in the second chamber are the most important factors). These exceptional circumstances have been discussed by a large literature and also found their way into formal models (e.g. Bräuninger and König 1999, Tsebelis 2002, Ganghof and Bräuninger 2006).

A central feature in determining policy production in European parliamentary democracies is coalition formation. Models of coalition formation usually focus on the political processes directly after the elections and assume rather implicitly how government will enact the policies agreed upon by the coalition partners. Laver and Shepsle (1996) introduce the idea of ministerial discretion in their coalition formation model. Principal-agent-problems that can arise from delegating power from the parliamentary parties to government are also subject to research. Martin and Vanberg (2005) deal with parliamentary scrutiny at the committee stage. Thies (2001) argues that junior ministers can take such control functions at an even earlier stage.

Such legislative models in parliamentary democracies have in common that they either focus exclusively on government or on the relationship between parliamentary majority and government. The standard day-to-day procedure of oppositional legislative activities in the first chamber has been largely neglected in the literature. In the remainder of this chapter, I will help close this gap and provide theoretical and empirical evidence for what motivates opposition parties to spend resources on a supposedly hopeless endeavor.

2.2 A Formal Model of Oppositional Bills as Policy Signals

The formal model of bill introduction constructed in the following represents the incentives of the central actors. It is intended to show formally that the puzzle of oppositional bill introduction dissolves when one focuses on the signaling of policy positions instead of on influence on policy output. Central empirical implications will be tested in the third part of this chapter.

The incentives of the actors can be represented as a simultaneous move game with complete but imperfect information. The players in the game are *government* and *opposition* acting as unitary actors. Government coalition C is composed of the two parties α and β whereas party γ forms the opposition. Party j ($j = \alpha, \beta, \gamma$) has the policy position p_{ij} on issue i ($i = 1, \ldots n$). While there is a multi-dimensional policy space, every issue i is assumed to be one-dimensional. Voters perceive the status quo sq on issue i, but they are unaware of each party's "true" policy position p_{ij}. Instead of observing the parties' policy positions directly, voters observe actual party activities from which they derive the positions. The activity modeled in this game is the parties' decision for one of the following actions: *introduce* legislation, or *refrain* from introducing legislation. By drafting a bill, parties commit a public signal of their policy position on the issue at hand. Figure 1 represents the game in extensive form.

Following Müller and Strøm (1999) I assume that parties want to reach certain goals: Parties want to maximize the votes they receive, they want to pursue certain policies, and/or they want to gain office. Sometimes these three goals are not compatible; sometimes they are conditional on each other. Influencing policy directly is difficult for opposition parties in most contexts in parliamentary democracies with a majority government. Therefore, opposition parties will rather have to focus on winning votes in order to improve their chances to gain office and finally implement policies.

Voters are assumed to follow a spatial logic: They support the party with the position closest to their ideal point on issue *i*. Voters are assumed not to know the position of parties on an issue until the party signals its position by introducing a bill. Voters' actual voting decision is not explicitly modeled here, but the overall evaluation of the parties is assumed to be a positive function of support on the individual issues. For the moment, parties are treated as unitary actors who have policy preferences on each issue *i*. These positions are treated as exogenous to the model. They could either be some aggregate of the individual positions of party members or MPs, or, to keep things easy, the position of the party leader. Hence, in the model parties do not choose their positions on the different issues opportunistically in order to maximize their expected number of votes, but they stick to their exogenously given position.[41] In order to win votes, however, it might be better not to openly pursue all policy goals a party agrees upon. Instead of changing its position in order to convince voters, a party can choose not to signal a position on a certain issue to the voters and instead focus on an issue on which it has a more popular position.[42] If a party signals its position on issue *i* by introducing a bill, the voters perceive this position and take this information into account for their voting decision. If government does not introduce a bill on issue *i*, the voters will assume that the government is happy with the status quo, which it decides not to change ($p_C = p_\alpha = p_\beta = sq$)[43]. Hence, in this case, the voters will perceive the status quo as the position of the government

41 In models of electoral competition in the Downsian tradition (Downs 1957), parties/MPs are assumed to follow an instrumental logic, adapting their policy positions in order to maximize votes. Models of legislative bargaining or coalition formation, on the contrary, typically assume that politicians attach some intrinsic value to policy. Such a behavior can be reasonably assumed if, for example, party members or long-term party supporters are alienated by suddenly shifting party positions. The same is true, if one presumes that party positions are some equilibrium position representing the aggregate of MPs' positions, which themselves represent constituency demands. The party position could, for instance, be represented by the median MP of the party who is elected party leader. In such a setting sudden shifts would meet the resistance of MPs whose constituency interests are in conflict with the new party position. More on the individual level perspective of bill introduction is discussed in Chapter 4. Benoit and Laver (2006) suggest reconciling the instrumental and the intrinsic logic of policy positions by distinguishing between "ideal" and "stated" policy positions. The logic of "stated" policy positions goes along perfectly with the idea of strategic signaling of policy positions developed below.

42 Compare Glazer and Lohmann (1999) for a similar argument of committing policy strategically from a government perspective.

43 Here and in the following, I omit the index *i* for the status quo and the actors' positions for reasons of readability. The index indicates that positions of parties and the status quo can differ over different issues.

parties on issue i. The same is true for the opposition party γ. If it does not reveal its true position on issue i by introducing a bill, the voters will assume that it supports the status quo ($p_\gamma = sq$). The situation differs if government introduces a bill and opposition does not. As the opposition refrains from signaling an alternative to the government's proposition which will alter the status quo, voters will assume that the opposition agrees with government on issue i ($p_\gamma = p_C$). Hence, voters will perceive the opposition's position to be identical with the position of the government bill, which will become the new status quo.

I assume that voters' ideal positions (p_v) are distributed uniformly over [0,1]. They support the party which is closest to their ideal point on issue i. If voters are indifferent between the positions of government and opposition on an issue, I assume that they will divide their support equally between all three parties. Voters are indifferent between the parties if their ideal position is located between the parties' positions or if the parties are perceived to hold the same ideal position. The latter scenario is the case if both government and opposition do not introduce a bill on an issue or if only government introduces a bill. I do not detail the voters' decision-making mechanism on which party to vote for on election day. The only assumption I make is that on average a party that finds support of a voter on issue i increases its chances of winning this voter's support at the voting booth. Hence, in order to win more voters than a competitor, a party has to engage in signaling policy positions distinct from its competitors. Only such a public controversy enables voters to make an informed choice. In such a setting, the coalition partners party α and party β cannot gain votes relative to each other on the field of legislation, at least as long as they act as an unitary actor in form of the government coalition C with a common position p_C, as assumed in the model.

The following pure strategies are available to government and opposition: *introduce* a bill or *refrain* from introducing a bill, $S_C = S_\gamma = \{\text{introduce, refrain}\}$. Party j's preferences are represented by a utility function that is an additive function of (1) the voter support that an actor's signaled position on issue i can generate (v_j), of (2) the costs of drafting the bill (c_jI, where I takes the value 1 if a bill is introduced and 0 if no bill is introduced), and of (3) the policy benefits ($F(|p_j - \omega|)$, where $F(.)$ is a monotonically increasing function) that the actor receives from the actual policy outcome ω: $u_j(s_C,s_\gamma) = v_j - c_jI - F(|p_j - \omega|)$.

Figure 1 A Model of Bill Introduction

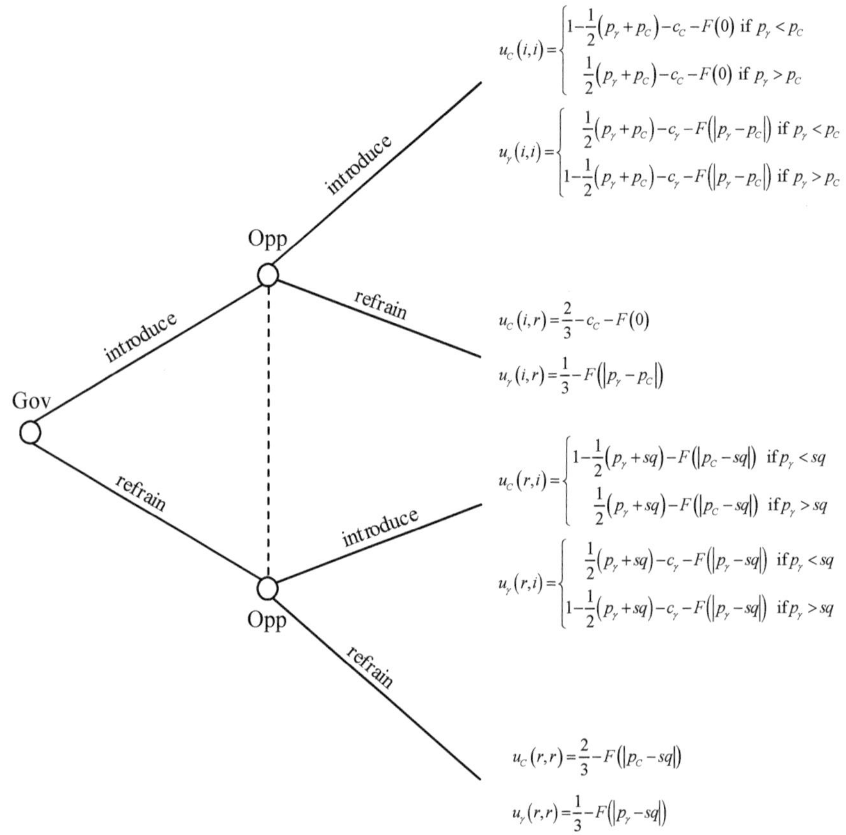

The number of voters who prefer the position of opposition over that of government or vice versa depends on the perceived positions of the parties. The perceived positions are a consequence of the strategies chosen and hence depend on the actions of both actors. If both actors do nothing *(r,r)*, or only government introduces a bill *(i,r)*, the voter support splits evenly between the three parties, hence $v_\alpha = v_\beta = \frac{1}{2} v_C = v_\gamma = \frac{1}{3}$. In all other strategy combinations the share of voters who support the party depends on the relative positions of both government and opposition, as is reflected by the utilities presented in Figure 1.

The factor c stands for the costs associated with bill introduction. The index j implies that the costs of bill introduction can differ between government and opposition.[44] The costs of bill introduction could be relatively cheaper for government as it can rely on more resources and experience in the ministries for drafting the bills. On the other hand, oppositional bills only intended as policy signals might not be as cost intensive as a "serious" policy proposal.

The policy term of the utility function is a positive, definite function of distance between the parties' ideal point and the policy outcome ω, which is either the status quo sq if the coalition C does not introduce a bill or the coalition position p_C if the coalition introduces a bill.[45] That is, the closer the actual outcome to the preferred policy, the higher a party's utility. This term does not play a role in strategic considerations of the opposition party, because its decision whether to introduce a bill or not does not influence the policy outcome. Hence, the term is a constant over all actions for the opposition.

The following Nash equilibria in pure strategies can be derived using best response functions of the players. The action profile s^* is a Nash equilibrium if and only if every player's action is a best response to the other player's action.

The best response of coalition C, when the opposition party γ refrains from introducing a bill, is easily derived as it is independent of the relative positions of the two actors and the status quo:

$$u_C(i,r) > u_C(r,r) \quad \text{if} \quad c_C < F(|p_C - sq|) - F(0) \qquad \text{I.}$$

That is, if opposition does not introduce a bill, it is worthwhile for government to initiate legislation on an issue as long as the costs of initiation are smaller than the policy loss from sticking with the status quo.

The other best responses are more complex, because they depend on the relative position of the status quo and/or the position of the other actor.

---

44 As mentioned before, the index i has been omitted here, as for all other factors, for reasons of readability. However, also between issues there should be differences depending on the complexity of the issue and the expertise that is available within a party.

45 In this model I assume that government bills always get adopted. Empirical evidence shows that this assumption reflects reality quite well: Government bills get adopted in the vast majority of cases. However, the legislation actually adopted does not necessarily reflect government's preferred policy p_C. Supermajority requirements or a situation of divided government might necessitate policy compromise. Such situations will be discussed below.

The opposition's best response to governmental inactivity is introducing a bill if the following conditions hold:

$$u_\gamma(r,i) > u_\gamma(r,r) \text{ if } \begin{cases} p_\gamma > \frac{2}{3} - sq + 2c_\gamma \ \ \& \ p_\gamma < sq \\ p_\gamma < \frac{4}{3} - sq - 2c_\gamma \ \ \& \ p_\gamma > sq \end{cases} \qquad \text{II.}$$

If government introduces a bill, opposition's utility from also introducing is higher than from not introducing, given the following inequality holds true:

$$u_\gamma(i,i) > u_\gamma(i,r) \text{ if } \begin{cases} p_\gamma > \frac{2}{3} - p_C + 2c_\gamma \ \ \& \ p_\gamma < p_C \\ p_\gamma < \frac{4}{3} - p_C - 2c_\gamma \ \ \& \ p_\gamma > p_C \end{cases} \qquad \text{III.}$$

For the opposition the policy gains or losses do not alter the strategic considerations because they are the same no matter what action the opposition chooses. Higher costs of bill introduction make it less likely for opposition to introduce a bill.

The government's best response to the opposition's decision to introduce a bill is defined by the most complex pattern, as the status quo as well as the position that party γ signals have to be considered:

$$u_C(i,i) > u_C(r,i) \text{ if } \begin{cases} p_C < sq + 2F(|p_C - sq|) - 2F(0) - 2c_C & \& \ p_\gamma < sq, p_C \\ p_C < 2 - 2p_\gamma - sq + 2F(|p_C - sq|) - 2F(0) - 2c_C & \& \ sq < p_\gamma < p_C \\ p_C > sq - 2F(|p_C - sq|) + 2F(0) + 2c_C & \& \ p_C, sq < p_\gamma \\ p_C > 2 - 2p_\gamma - sq - 2F(|p_C - sq|) + 2F(0) + 2c_C & \& \ p_C < p_\gamma < sq \end{cases} \qquad \text{IV.}$$

In addition to the relative position of government, of the opposition, and of the status quo, also the costs of bill introduction, as well as the policy costs of not introducing a bill are important for the strategic decisions of government. It holds that government is less likely to introduce a bill if the costs of bill introduction exceed the policy costs of not introducing. Or, more generally, larger costs of bill introduction make bill introduction less likely, whereas a larger distance between the status quo and the government's ideal point encourages legislative activities of government.

The game has Nash equilibria if the action of government is a best response to the action of opposition and vice versa, formally if $s_C^* = b(s_\gamma^*) \,\&\, s_\gamma^* = b(s_C^*)$.

There are five different possible scenarios: A Nash equilibrium in pure strategies in which (1) both introduce a bill, $s^*(i,i)$ (if III and VI hold simultaneously), where (2) only government introduces a bill, $s^*(i,r)$ (if I holds and III does not hold), where (3) only opposition introduces a bill, $s^*(r,i)$ (if II holds and IV does not hold), where (4) both actors refrain from introducing, $s^*(r,r)$ (if I and II do not hold), and finally, a scenario in which (5) there is no Nash equilibrium in pure strategies (if I and II, I and III, II and IV, or III and not IV hold, and at the same time none of the other combinations mentioned above holds).[46]

Figure 2 shows the equilibrium strategies for all possible combinations of positions of government and opposition for different positions of the status quo.[47] For the depiction of the Nash equilibrium strategies, the cost factors c_C and c_γ are set to be zero, or at least to be smaller than the policy benefits for government, which are supposed to be smaller than the loss of one vote $(0 \leq c_C < F(|\, p_C - sq\,|) - F(0) < |\, v_j' - v_j\,|)$. Given these assumptions, government always has an incentive to legislate if opposition does nothing.[48] In all other cases, the strategic considerations are solely based on the vote-winning potential of bill introduction.

---

46 If the game were modeled differently, actors could realize Pareto improvements over the status quo in some of these situations. Instead of having both actors decide simultaneously, one could allow the actors to make binding commitments to overcome coordination problems. In such a game government and opposition could make a binding commitment, and, for instance, introduce a bill together, in cases in which both would fare better from introducing a bill if the other one does not introduce a bill with a different position. To give a numerical example for such a situation: The coalition C agrees on the position $p_C = 0.2$, the opposition party has the position $p_\gamma = 0.25$. The status quo lies at $sq = 1/3$. If the opposition does not introduce a bill, government has an incentive to introduce if the policy gains are greater than the costs of drafting a bill. If opposition introduces a bill, government prefers not to signal its position as a majority of voters likes the status quo better. Opposition has an incentive to introduce a bill only if government introduces a bill (as the majority of voters prefer its position over governments' position but not over the status quo), and if the benefits in votes outweigh the costs for drafting. The payoff structure leads to a situation where no Nash equilibrium in pure strategies exists. However, if both actors could agree on introducing a bill together with the position of government, they could both profit from policy gains, share the costs of bill introduction, and risk no punishment by the voters as these are not presented with a better alternative.

47 Only the status quo positions 0, 0.25, 1/3, and 0.5 are presented. If the status quo is bigger than 0.5 the same logic applies, however, insofar as the results are mirror images of Figure 2.

48 This explains why the scenario in which no one introduces a bill is not represented in this figure.

Figure 2 Equilibrium Strategies for Government and Opposition

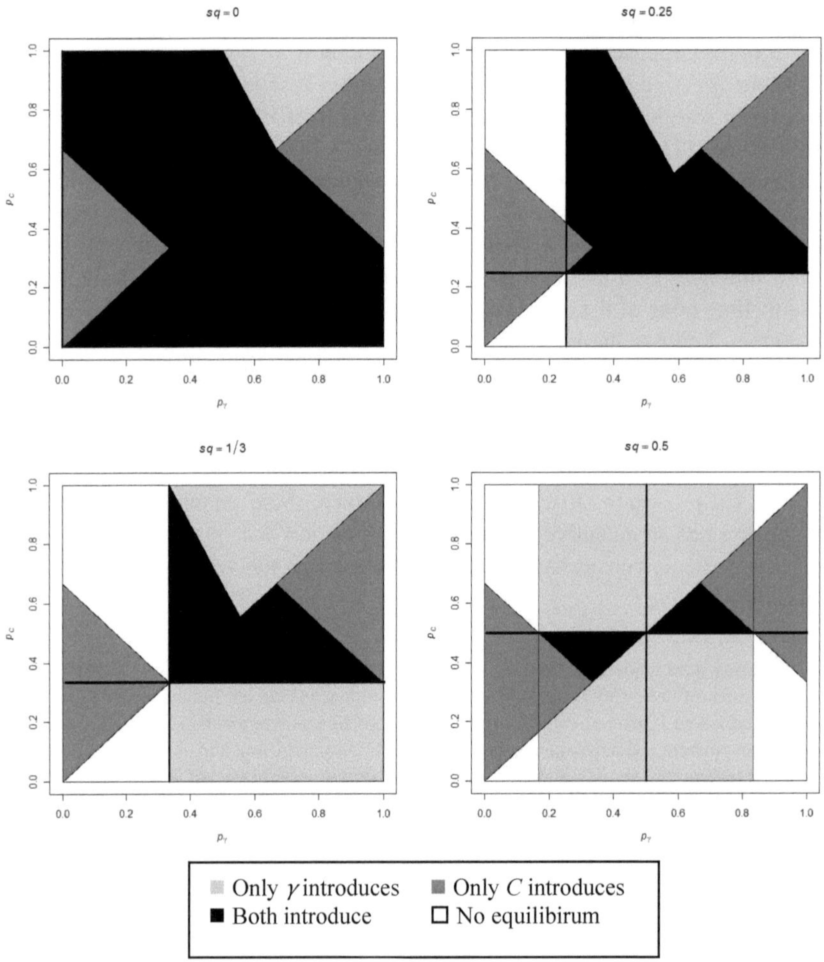

As becomes evident from the above model, the more radical the status quo, the more likely that both government and opposition will introduce a bill signaling their own position. For more moderate positions of the status quo, the introduction of a government and an opposition bill on the same issue is less likely. When government has a central position on an issue, it is less likely that opposition will introduce a bill alone. When opposition has a central position on an issue, it is always worthwhile signaling this position to the voters. Radical positions should foremost be signaled if the status quo is quite radical and if the opposition party opposes government on the issue.

The following hypotheses on the importance of the relative positions of the actors and the status quo can thus be derived:

Hypothesis 1 The more central the position of an actor, the more likely it is that the actor introduces a bill on the issue.

Hypothesis 2 The more extreme the status quo, the more likely it is that each actor will introduce a bill.

Even though oppositional bill sponsorship activities were modeled as being driven by vote-seeking considerations, the oppositional activities also have indirect policy effects: The competition for votes will reduce radical policy proposals by government when the fear to lose voters to a more moderate opposition exceeds the policy gains from a radical policy shift.

The influence of the cost factors also has empirical implications:

Hypothesis 3 The larger the distance between the status quo and the government position on an issue, the more likely it is that government will introduce a bill.

Hypothesis 4 The more costly it is for an actor to draft a bill on an issue, the fewer bills the actor will introduce.

So far I have only discussed the implications of the simple model for the case of a government coalition acting as a unitary actor, which gets all bills adopted, and one opposition party. In order to make the model more realistic some of the assumptions could be modified. In the following, I will discuss such modifications and their implications.

In this game government has been so far perceived as a unitary actor introducing a bill according to its ideal point. However, the position of minimal winning coalition governments is a compromise needing the support of all coalition partners. These veto players (Tsebelis 2002) within the coalition can prevent a common position that is necessary for changing the status quo.[49] If government

[49] In this context I focus on the failure of forming a common position prior to bill introduction. Alternatively, the control that government compromise does not deviate too far from the party

cannot agree on a common position, the whole game is reduced to a one-player game, where opposition follows a decision theoretic logic: The decision whether to introduce a bill or not only depends on the position of the opposition relative to the status quo. If the utility derived from introducing a bill on a given issue is higher than from not introducing a bill, opposition will come forward with a bill. The utility from introducing is equivalent to the utility $u_\gamma(r,i)$ and $u_\gamma(r,r)$, respectively. It can be seen from Figure 2 that opposition will sometimes introduce a bill if signaling its position can win more votes than being associated with the status quo, but sometimes it will also refrain in such a case, depending on the position of government. If government is unable to interfere, overall oppositional bill introduction becomes more likely. Following the assumptions of veto player theory, it is more likely that government cannot agree on a common position the more coalition partners there are and the further apart their positions are. This leads to the following hypothesis:

> *Hypothesis 5* If government cannot agree on a common position on a certain issue, it is more likely that opposition will introduce a bill on the issue.

It has also been assumed so far that government always gets its common ideal position p_C adopted. As has been discussed in Chapter 1 of this study, it is a reasonable assumption that government bills get adopted, however, it is not necessarily the case that they reflect the government ideal point. A strong second chamber with an opposing majority or supermajority requirements might force government to introduce bills that reflect policy compromises with the opposition already at the stage of introduction (Manow and Burkhart 2007) or bills that are getting amended in the legislative process. The implications of such situations are more difficult to see. Policy payoffs for the government as a unitary actor are lower when the outcome does not reflect the ideal position anymore. Such a compromise position, however, might even convince more voters than the pure government policy. If one regards the coalition partners as individual actors, the policy payoffs of a compromise with opposition might be higher for one partner and lower for the other partner. Hence, for such situations empirical implications cannot be easily derived. In some situations government might be keen on introducing policy compromises with opposition, in other situations the need of getting the consent of opposition parties might rather reduce government's legislative productivity.

line of the coalition partners could also take place in parliament. Through amendments in the committee stage the content of bills could be changed (Martin and Vanberg 2005) or a coalition partner could vote against a legislative project in the final vote on a bill.

The formal model developed above shows that vote-seeking incentives are a potential explanation for oppositional bill sponsorship. An empirical test of the model meets some difficulties: First, the model assumes a governing coalition of two parties and one opposition party as actors. Adding additional coalition partners does not change the predicted equilibrium strategies as long as the government acts as a unitary actor. On the other hand, if one understands the coalition partners as veto players, additional veto players would increase the likelihood of policy stability. If coalition partners are not modeled as veto players, but are assumed to form their position as some kind of weighted average of their individual ideal points, radical positions would become less likely with an increasing number of coalition partners. However, necessary side payments in order to get to a common position might again make policy change less likely.

More problematic for the predictions of the model would be a higher number of opposition parties, which would make the game much more complex. In such a setup, for example, the centrality of an actor is not necessarily a good thing for winning votes anymore. An actor who is closely framed by two competitors would only be left with few votes. In this case refraining from bill introduction in order to be associated with a more radical status quo could be the better strategic choice. But the strategic constellation of two camps of competitors is not necessarily unrealistic. In Germany, the constellation of two coalition parties and one opposition party describes the political reality of a long period quite well. Even when the Green party entered the Bundestag in 1983 the strategic constellation did not change radically, as there were now two blocks of left and right parties which would compete against each other. Neither do more complex situations necessarily require giving up the simple model. Often the competition for votes on a certain issue will not involve all parties. Instead, the government will be confronted with one opposition party that cares especially about the issue at hand. In such situations other parties might not consider introducing a bill even if their position could attract voters, as the costs of drafting a bill on an issue on which the party has no expertise exceeds potential vote gains. In addition, open competition for votes usually takes place between government and opposition parties and not within government and opposition. Consequently, the hypotheses are expected to hold in a larger variety of cases. In the following, I will test the empirical implications of the theoretical model.

2.3 Comparative Evidence for Bills as Strategic Policy Signals

In this section, I analyze whether government and opposition use bills strategically to send policy signals on issues where they can maximize their utility. Strategic employment of bills as described in the theoretical model would suggest that parties signal their position especially on issues on which they can win most votes, where costs are low, and, in the case of government, where the expected policy gains are the highest. In the following, I will present empirical evidence for the above hypotheses by examining data from Belgium, France, Germany, and the United Kingdom.

2.3.1 Data and Measurements

The data used for the analysis stems from the project "Comparative Legislation" for which data on all bills introduced over several legislative periods in Belgium, France, Germany, and the United Kingdom has been collected from official sources. The time period covered differs between the selected countries: For France, data between 1986 and 2002 was available, for the United Kingdom between 1987 and 2003. For Belgium, newer data could be used (1988-2007), whereas in the German case data reaching further back in time was used (1976-2002).[50]

In an ideal research design the position of all actors on every issue that could lead to potential legislative action would be measured along with their decision to introduce a legislative proposal on that specific issue or not. As this procedure is hardly possible, I identify a number of central policy dimensions for each country and analyze how many bills a party has introduced on that policy dimension in a certain legislative period. The number of bills introduced should depend among other things on the centrality of the party's position, the position of the status quo, and the costs associated with introducing bills on a certain policy dimension.

The dependent variable is operationalized as the number of bills introduced by a political actor (government, parliamentary majority, or an individual party) per legislative period on a certain policy dimension. I distinguish between an economic, a social, and an environmental policy dimension in all four countries. Additionally, a fourth policy dimension "Decentralization" is taken into account in Belgium and the United Kingdom, where regional or even separatist tenden-

---

[50] For Germany, data from Bräuninger and König (2000) was used in addition to the "Comparative Legislation" data. The data reaching further back in time is based on the same source as the "Comparative Legislation" data.

cies play an important role in political competition. Bills were assigned to the policy dimensions in a two step procedure. In a first step, bills were assigned to policy categories which were constructed based on the German committee and ministry structure. The leading committee in which a bill is dealt with, or the portfolio of the minister who has primary responsibility of introducing the bill, determines to which policy category the bill belongs. For coding the bills in the other four countries, these policy categories were completed with two additional categories for "Regionalization" and "Europeanization" to cover policy categories of special importance in the respective countries. Especially in the United Kingdom with its "devolution" and in Belgium with the ongoing conflict between the language communities, the issue of regionalization and decentralization are central issues of political conflict. The policy categories of the Belgian bills were coded based on the "eurovoc"-codes in the official data base. For the French and British bills, hand-coding of bill titles and short descriptions of the bills were necessary.

In a second step, the policy categories were aggregated into policy dimensions for which policy positions of actors can be assigned (compare Table 4). Bills falling into the policy categories "Defense", "Foreign Affairs", "Europe", and "Communication, Media, Film, Sport" were neglected in the further analysis: Concerning the first three categories, there are only very few parliamentary initiatives as matters related to foreign affairs are usually perceived as the domain of government. Likewise, the category "Communication, Media, Film, Sport" was not taken into account as it comprises bills with very different policy aspects that cannot be assigned to one specific dimension.

Table 4 Assignment of Policy Categories to Policy Dimensions

Economic	Social	Environmental	Regionalization
Economic Affairs and Energy, Finance, Education, Science and Research	Interior, Justice, Social Affairs	Traffic, Mobility, Construction, Health, Consumer Protection, Environment, Animal Protection, Agriculture	Regionalization

In the analysis conducted below the focus is on the strategic behavior of government and individual opposition parties. Therefore "cross-bench" or "mixed" bills, that is, bills that were introduced jointly by government and opposition parties are excluded from the analysis (compare Bräuninger and Debus 2010 for an analysis of this type of bills).[51] Joint bills among government parties or among opposition parties were likewise neglected, as the cooperation in bill introduction cannot be explained with a model that suggests that signaling the party position is the primary goal of oppositional bill introduction. For these bills other explanations have to be found. The only exception is Germany, where the government parties almost exclusively sponsor parliamentary initiatives together. These bills were taken into account in the analysis. Overall, however, bills introduced by more than one party (or MPs from different parties) within the government or the opposition camp are minor in number. They only make up around one percent of all parliamentary bills in France. Within the German opposition cooperation is even rarer than in France: Less than one percent of all opposition bills are the result of cooperation between different opposition parties. In the United Kingdom, such cooperation within the House of Commons does not exist due to the fact that only one MP per chamber signs responsible for a bill. In Belgium, co-operation within the government camp is more frequent (15 percent of the bills introduced by coalition parties) than among opposition parties (four percent of all opposition bills).

The central independent variables that are used in order to test empirically the hypotheses derived above are based on positional information on the parties and government. The positions of these actors are measured using computerized textual analysis. The wordscores method (Laver et al. 2003) allows for determining the policy positions of different texts. With the help of reference texts with known positions, so-called virgin texts with unknown positions are scored. The wordscores technique has been applied in a number of contexts usually to find the positions of party manifestos (e.g. Benoit and Laver 2003, Debus 2008, Bräuninger and Debus 2012) or political speeches (e.g. Laver and Benoit 2002, Gianetti and Laver 2005, Bernauer and Bräuninger 2009). As I assume that bills contain policy signals that reflect the policy signals revealed by election manifestos, I use the election manifestos of the election prior to the legislative period under discussion in order to derive the policy positions assumably signaled in the bills. For Belgian and German governments coalition agreements were used to obtain government positions. The positions of the governments of the United Kingdom were based on the so-called Queen's speeches. For France, where no direct measure of the government position was available, the government posi-

[51] Such cooperation between government and opposition within the first chamber is almost non-existent in France and the United Kingdom (in the latter case bills are only introduced by individual MPs, therefore "cross-bench" cooperation can only take place between the House of Commons and the House of Lords, which is, however, only rarely the case). In Germany and Belgium, such cooperation takes place more often, yet these bills only constitute nine and seven percent of all parliamentary bills.

tion was assumed to lie at the "center of gravity" (compare Gross and Sigelman 1984, and Cusack 2001 and Bräuninger 2005 for applications of this concept), that is, the weighted average position of the coalition partners.[52]

The party manifestos of the elections closest to the data collection period of the reference values are used as reference texts. The reference values on the selected policy dimensions are drawn from expert survey data by Laver and Hunt (1992) for the earlier years and Benoit and Laver (2006) for the more recent elections.[53] The reason for using reference texts early and late in the observation periods is to control for changes in the meaning of words and to allow for new topics that enter the political agenda. The party manifestos in the other election years as well as the coalition agreements and Queen's speeches serve as so-called virgin texts and are scored using these pieces of information.[54]

The degree to which the parties represented in parliament are covered in the subsequent analysis differs between countries. In Germany, data on all parties represented in parliament is available. In the other selected countries, independents and representatives of minor parties had to be excluded from the analysis as no party manifestos for these representatives were available. Another reason for the exclusion of minor parties is that the theoretical model only covers parties that intend to compete with government on a broad range of issues and does not take into account parties with special narrow policy interests, which target just a small part of the electorate.[55]

---

52 In the period studied here there are two cases of changes in the party composition of government during the legislative period: In Germany, the coalition of SPD and FDP under Chancellor Helmut Schmidt broke down in September 1982 and was replaced by a coalition of CDU/CSU and FDP under Chancellor Helmut Kohl in October of the same year. New elections were held in March 1983. The bills introduced during the few months in-between October and March were not considered in the analysis. The same is true for the French case, when in 1988 Prime Minister Jacques Chirac resigned after having lost the presidential election. The caretaker government, which was in office until the early elections, was not considered in the analysis.

53 The policy dimensions are operationalized as follows in the surveys. Economic policy: Increase service vs. cut taxes; Social policy: Promote permissive social policy vs. do not promote; Environmental policy: Environment over growth vs. growth over environment; Decentralization policy: Pro vs. anti decentralization of decisions.

54 The political documents can be retrieved from the open access archive of political documents polidoc.net (Benoit et al. 2009).

55 In the case of the United Kingdom information was available on the three largest parties Conservatives, Labour, and Liberal Democrats, as well as for the Scottish National Party and the Welsh party Plaid Cymru. Other small parties with only few representatives could not be considered due to lacking party manifestos (this concerns the Social Democratic Party, the Ulster Unionist Party, the Ulster Democratic Party, and Sinn Féin; the latter followed a policy of abstentionism, that is, elected members of Sinn Féin did not take their seats in the House of Commons and consequently did not introduce legislation). The same holds true for independents.

The central independent variables in order to test the hypotheses empirically are first, the centrality of the political actors (Hypothesis 1), and second, the centrality of the status quo (Hypothesis 2). In addition, government should be more active if the distance between its policy ideal point and the status quo is larger (Hypothesis 3), and the number of bills should be lower for any actor if the costs of introduction are higher (Hypothesis 4). The centrality of actors is measured as their absolute distance to the position of the median party. When a single party has the absolute majority in parliament, as is the case in the United Kingdom during the entire period of observation, this party's position constitutes the median position on all policy dimensions. When coalitions are necessary to form a majority government, the median position can be held by different (governing or opposition) parties on the different dimensions. As I have no information on the position of the status quo, I assume that the status quo lies at the ideal point of the previous government. The centrality of the status quo is measured as its absolute distance to the median party on each dimension. The distance of an actor to the status quo is measured as the absolute distance between an actor's ideal point and the status quo as defined above.

The costs for introducing bills are operationalized as follows: I assume that parties have a higher expertise on issues that are important to them, therefore it should be cheaper for them to introduce bills concerning policy dimensions with a high saliency for the party. The saliency measures are also derived using wordscores based on party manifestos, coalition agreements, and Queen's speeches with reference values taken from the expert surveys (Laver and Hunt 1992 and Benoit and Laver 2006). The size of a parliamentary party group should also influence the costs of bill introduction. In larger parties, the preparation of bills can be divided between a larger number of MPs, hence the individual costs of bill introduction should be lower. To account for the decreasing marginal benefits of party size, I take the logarithm of the seat share of a party group or government. Another factor making bills more expensive for government could be the level of disagreement between the coalition partners. Larger policy differences on a certain policy dimension could necessitate high side payments in order to come to a common policy proposal. If coalition partners act as veto players (Hypothesis 5) it might also be the case that policy change on a certain dimension becomes unlikely when the distance between the coalition partners is very large. In such a case the probability of oppositional bills would increase.

Taken together, the group of MPs that had to be left out in the analysis is responsible for only one bill per year on average. In Belgium and France, too, independents were excluded from the analysis.

Descriptive statistics of the dependent and independent variables used in the regressions can be found in Table 6 in the Appendix to this chapter.

The question of how the parties of the parliamentary majority behave in the legislative game has not been explicitly dealt with in the theoretical model. I will therefore treat it as an empirical question whether the parliamentary majority follows more closely the strategic considerations of government, seeing bills as a means to influence policy, or whether government parties react more like opposition in order to send independent policy signals.

2.3.2 Statistical Model

The dependent variable has a discrete count structure. Count data has certain properties that require special econometric treatment: It is intrinsically heteroskedastic, non-negative, right-skewed, and has a variance that increases with the mean of the distribution (Hilbe 2007: 8). Not considering the specific count structure of the data can lead to inefficient, inconsistent, and biased estimates. The basic model to deal with these properties is the Poisson regression model that is a generalized linear model based on the univariate Poisson distribution: $\Pr(y \mid \mu) = \frac{e^{-\mu}\mu^{y}}{y!}$ for $y = 0,1,2,3,\ldots$, where μ is the expected number of times an event will occur over a given period and y a random variable indicating the number of times an event did occur (Long and Freese 2006: 349). In this distribution $\mu > 0$ is the only parameter that defines the distribution. The Poisson regression model is an extension of the univarite Poisson distribution as it allows each observation to have a different value μ. The mean μ_i is estimated using the independent variables for each observation i: $\mu_i = Var(y_i \mid x_i) = E(y_i \mid xi) = \exp(x_i\beta)$.

However, this classical count model has one big disadvantage, as it relies on the assumption of equidispersion, which means that the mean and the variance are equal. Most real world data violates this assumption. This is also true for the data analyzed here. The more general negative binomial regression model allows for overdispersion – a conditional variance larger than the conditional mean – in the data. The Poisson regression model and the negative binomial regression model have the same mean structure, but the variance structure of the latter model is as follows: $Var(y_i \mid x_i) = \mu_i + \alpha\mu_i^2$. It can be easily seen that the negative binomial regression model is reduced to the Poisson regression model when $\alpha = 0$. Likelihood ratio tests show that α is significantly different from 0 for all models presented below. I decided against pooling the data from the different countries as the differences in the legislative process, the electoral system, and the party system make it likely that the effects of the variables differ largely between the countries. Further, the positional data is not necessarily comparable between the countries.

2.3.3 Empirical Results

Table 5 presents the results of the negative binomial regression models with the number of bills per policy dimension a party or government introduced. The likelihood ratio χ^2 tests for all models show that the joint effect of all variables in these models is greater than zero. The choice of the negative binomial regression model over the Poisson regression model is justified by the fact that α is significantly larger than zero in all models. The fact that some of the coefficients have different signs over the different countries lends support to the decision to analyze the countries separately.

There is limited empirical evidence for the theoretical model. The findings concerning the distance of an actor to the median legislator are in line with Hypothesis 1 in most cases. In Belgium, France, and Germany, it holds that if the distance to the median increases on the relevant policy dimension, the number of bills introduced on that dimension decreases. The effect reaches the highest level of statistical significance and is strongest in relative terms in Germany, where a one unit increase in distance leads to a nine percent decrease in the expected number of bills. For the Flemish parties in Belgium, the coefficient has the expected sign but is not statistically significant. In the United Kingdom, where we have the special case that the government party represents the median on all policy dimensions, the effect is statistically insignificant and has a positive sign.

There is no empirical evidence in the model that the extremity of the status quo, measured as the distance between the position of the government in the previous legislative period and the current median legislator, leads to an increase in the legislative activities of all actors (Hypothesis 2). The coefficient has the wrong sign in four out of five regressions and is statistically insignificant in all five regressions. Also the distance of an actor to the status quo does not have the predicted effect. It was expected that government should be more active if the status quo is further away, because the policy costs imposed by the unsatisfying status quo are higher (Hypothesis 3). For the opposition no such effect was expected, as opposition bills are unlikely to change the status quo and therefore cannot change the policy costs. However, these effects cannot be found in the data.

Table 5 Negative Binomial Regression Results for the Number of Bills Introduced per Policy Dimension by Parliamentary Actors

	Belgium (Walloon Parties)	Belgium (Flemish Parties)	France	Germany	UK
Distance of Actor	-0.067**	-0.038	-0.055*	-0.089***	0.043
to Median	(0.03)	(0.03)	(0.03)	(0.03)	(0.03)
Distance of SQ	-0.014	0.005	-0.035	-0.023	-0.011
to Median	(0.05)	(0.03)	(0.06)	(0.03)	(0.04)
Distance of Actor	0.018	0.053	0.006	0.042**	0.012
to SQ	(0.04)	(0.03)	(0.03)	(0.02)	(0.03)
Distance of Actor	-0.029	-0.134	-0.107	-0.005	0.105
to SQ X Gov.	(0.10)	(0.10)	(0.08)	(0.04)	(0.08)
Distance of Actor	-0.002	-0.083*	0.017	0.035	0.035
to SQ X Parl. Maj.	(0.05)	(0.05)	(0.05)	(0.04)	(0.06)
Salience of Policy	0.087***	0.109***	-0.033	0.050**	0.106***
Dimension	(0.02)	(0.02)	(0.04)	(0.02)	(0.03)
Seat Share of Actor	0.915***	0.326***	0.793***	0.017	0.900***
(Logarithm)	(0.09)	(0.08)	(0.09)	(0.07)	(0.06)
Maximal Dist. in	-0.010	-0.009	0.079*	0.036	
Coalition	(0.02)	(0.02)	(0.04)	(0.02)	
Maximal Dist. in	0.015	0.037	-0.105	-0.013	
Coalition X Gov.	(0.03)	(0.04)	(0.07)	(0.03)	
Maximal Dist. in	0.047	0.024	-0.055	-0.009	
Coal. X Parl. Maj.	(0.03)	(0.03)	(0.07)	(0.04)	
Government	-0.586*	0.532*	0.011	1.261***	-0.768***
	(0.32)	(0.30)	(0.66)	(0.21)	(0.27)
Parliamentary	-1.289***	-0.151	-0.454	-0.023	-0.165
Majority	(0.25)	(0.24)	(0.42)	(0.24)	(0.30)
Economic	3.035***	2.877***	1.307***	0.537***	1.468***
Dimension	(0.22)	(0.21)	(0.36)	(0.11)	(0.20)
Social	3.437***	3.367***	2.324***	0.642***	1.947***
Dimension	(0.22)	(0.19)	(0.36)	(0.13)	(0.19)

Environmental Dimension	2.132*** (0.21)	2.250*** (0.22)			1.962*** (0.17)
Constant	-4.950*** (0.41)	-7.285*** (0.46)	-2.467*** (0.41)	-5.399*** (0.37)	-5.959*** (0.49)
α	0.248***	0.212***	0.342***	0.091***	0.114***
Pseudo R^2	0.215	0.204	0.150	0.180	0.275
LR χ^2	231.97***	236.06***	108.81***	138.34***	197.97***
N	128	132	72	87	96

Note: Days in parliament as exposure time, opposition party as reference category, environmental dimension as reference policy dimension for Germany and France, regionalization as reference policy dimension for Belgium and the United Kingdom; * significant at 10 percent ** at 5 percent *** at 1 percent; standard errors in parentheses.

The other cost variables provide good evidence for the expectations formulated in Hypothesis 4: With the exception of France, the expected positive relationship between saliency of a policy dimension and number of bills initiated can be found in all countries. Similarly, the effect that larger party groups introduce more bills is found in all countries but Germany.

The distance between the coalition partners seems to have no clear effects on legislative productivity in most countries. Only in France evidence in line with Hypothesis 5 is found, namely, that larger policy differences between the coalition partners make oppositional activities more likely. Institutional effects seem to drive the effects of the variable controlling for government and parliamentary majority. For the policy dimension dummies the expected signs can be found. Keeping everything else equal, more economic and social bills than environmental bills are introduced in Germany and France, and in Belgium and the United Kingdom bills on the regionalization dimension are the least frequent.

The central findings are robust to a number of variations in the model specification. Adding period dummies to control for level differences in the number of bills sponsored in the different periods hardly affects the results. All central variables keep their statistical significance and also the size of the coefficients varies only to a small degree. The only remarkable difference in the period dummy model is that further evidence against Hypothesis 3 is found. For France, the interaction term between the distance of an actor to the status quo and the government dummy has now a statistically significant negative effect, whereas, comparable to German opposition parties, the results for Walloon opposition parties reveal an unexpected positive effect. The findings presented above are also confirmed when one controls for the violation of the assumption that observations are independent by allowing for legislative period clusters. With robust standard errors for dependence of observations within one legislative period, the effect of the distance to the median legislator is now statistically significant for all countries. In addition, the negative effect of the distance between government coalition partners on their legislative productivity is now statistically significant for France.

2.3.4 Discussion

Figure 3 through Figure 5 graphically display the central effects found in the empirical analyses. The figures show the effects that the distance of an actor to the median voter, the salience of a policy dimension, and a party's seat share exert on the expected number of bills introduced. For the baseline models an opposition party is assumed, hence, the dummies controlling for the government and the parliamentary majority, as well as the variables interacted with these dummies, are set to zero. The other variables are held constant at their mean. The dashed lines show 80 percent confidence intervals.

When looking at the three figures provided here it is remarkable that always one country falls out of the general picture. In Figure 3 all countries but the United Kingdom show the expected effect that a larger distance to the median legislator decreases the legislative activities of a party. As the predictions of the formal model cannot be applied one to one, this finding is not problematic. The United Kingdom has a special situation with single-party majority governments. Here, government and parliamentary majority automatically represent the median legislator on all policy dimensions. Consequently, this variable also captures government-opposition differences to some extent. Overall, the findings can thus be taken as evidence for Hypothesis 1 derived from the theoretical model.

The non-findings concerning the absolute position of the status quo (Hypothesis 2) and the relative position of the status quo (Hypothesis 3), however, casts some doubt on the overall predictive power of the model. One reason for the rejection of the two hypotheses might be the oversimplification of the policy-making process in the model. Contrary to the model assumptions, government does not always get what it wants. Consequently, the potential policy gains might be overestimated when operationalizing the status quo position as the position of the predecessor government.

Figure 3 Expected Number of Bills as a Function of Distance to the Median Legislator

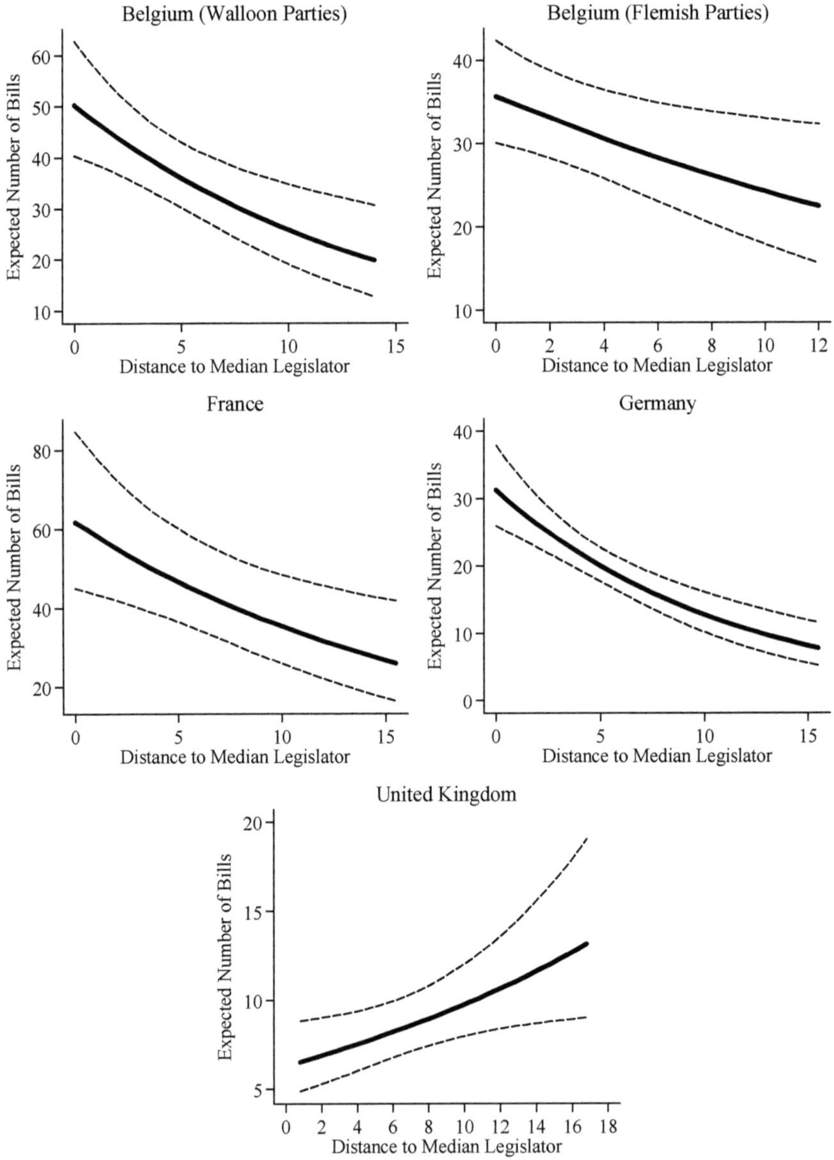

Figure 4 Expected Number of Bills as a Function of Salience

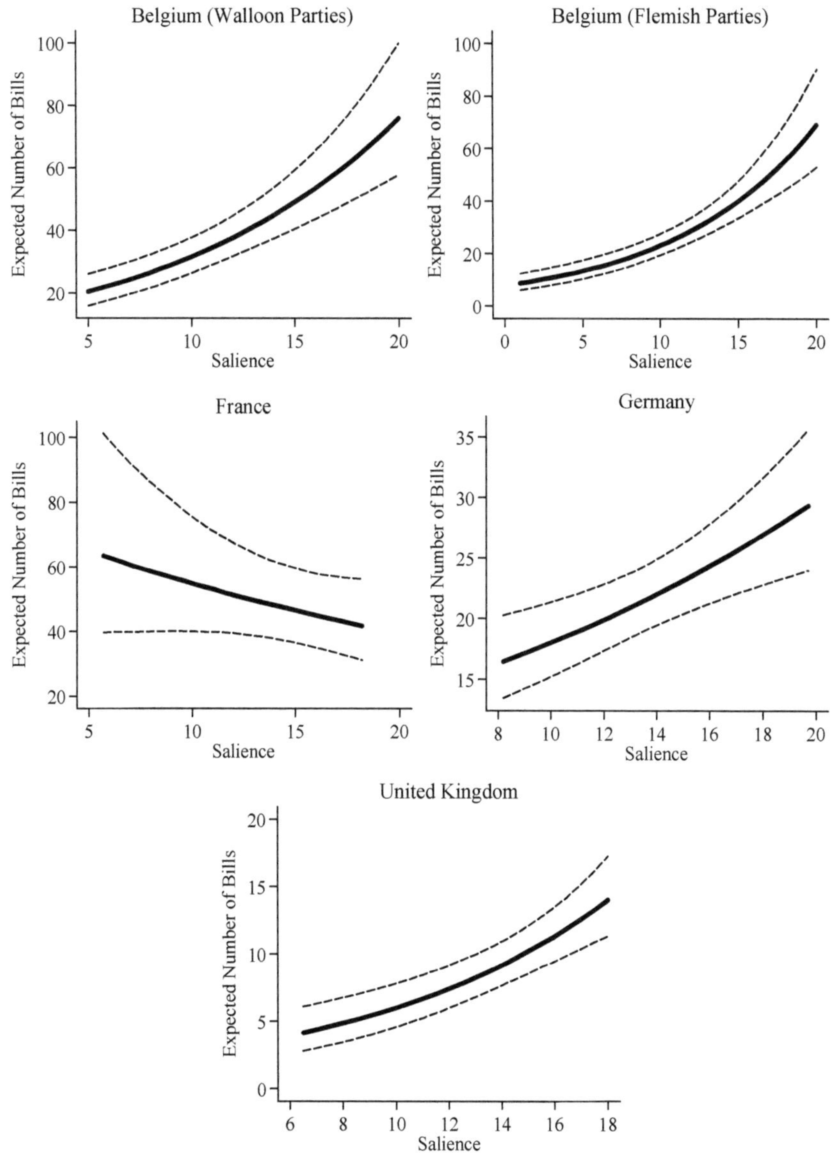

Figure 5 Expected Number of Bills as a Function of Party Seat Share

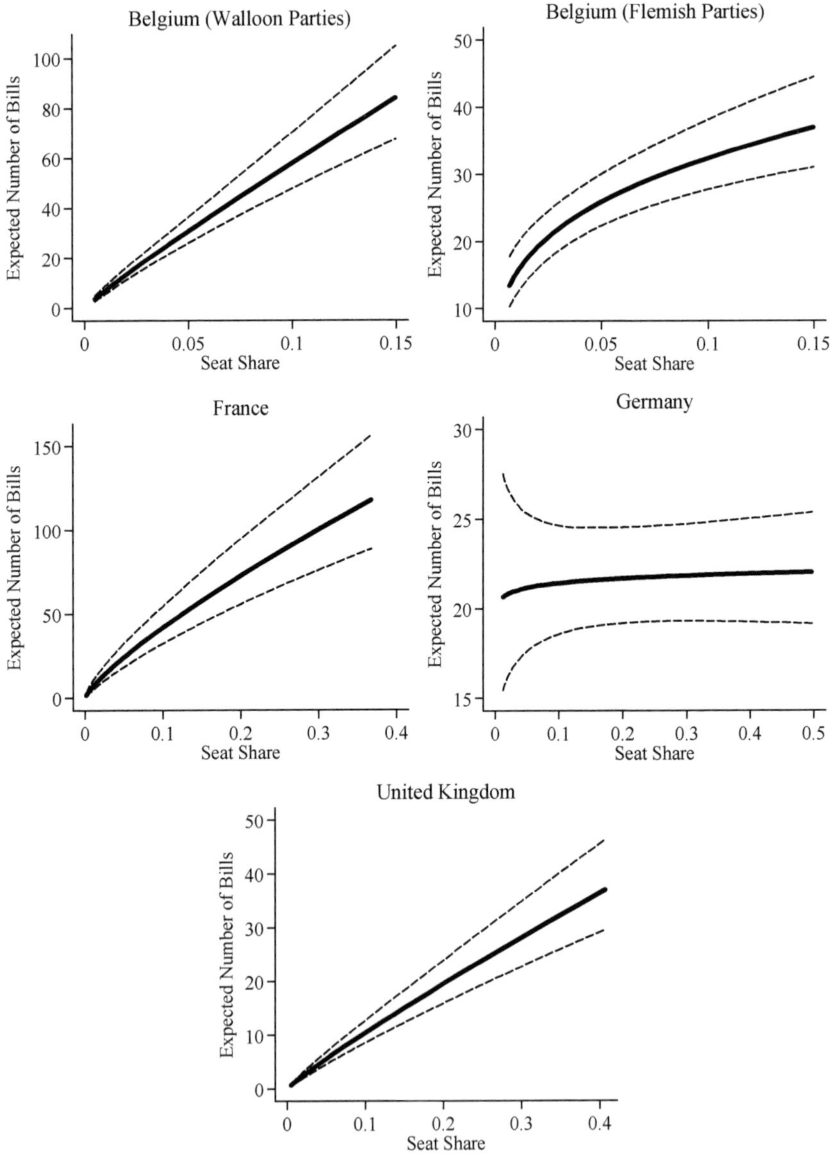

In the United Kingdom, with its prototype majoritarian system (Lijphart 1999), where governments are assumed to have the greatest possibilities to realize their agenda, this operationalization should work best. Here, the coefficients of the variables employed for testing Hypothesis 3 have the predicted sign but fail statistical significance. For Hypothesis 5 (that a larger distance between coalition partners makes oppositional bill introduction more likely) at best limited evidence is found in France.

The hypotheses concerning the cost factors also apply to the United Kingdom. In contrast to the positional variables, the variables measuring Hypothesis 4 have statistically significant effects in the United Kingdom, indicating that actors introduce more bills on more salient policy dimensions, and they also introduce more bills the larger the party group. These effects can also be found in most other countries. In France, however, there is no evidence for more bill introduction on salient policy dimensions. On the contrary, the coefficient of this statistically insignificant variable even has a negative sign. This could indicate that the programmatic interests and expertise of the party play a less important role than in the other countries. Individual motives for bill introduction independent of salience might be more important in the French context. French MPs might pursue an individual agenda, which reflects constituency interests that differ from issues that party deems important. Or, if they have a personal vote-seeking interest in introducing bills, they might choose issues that do not to interfere with the party line.

The odd one out concerning the seat share variable is Germany. Here, no positive effect of the size of government or of a party group on the number of bills can be found. Germany differs from the other countries in two respects concerning the size of party groups. On the one hand, the five percent threshold excludes independents and small splitter parties from parliament. Additionally and probably more importantly, bill introduction is a collective right in the German Bundestag. Even small party groups seem to have enough resources to cover all the issues they want to cover so that size does not matter. The substantial effect the seat share variable has in the other countries (it has the most extreme effect in France, where the smallest party groups are expected to introduce close to no bill at all, whereas large party groups are expected to sponsor more than 100 bills per legislative period and dimension) might point to something else: Maybe a larger seat share has more meaning than just reducing the costs of introduction for a party group. If bills also serve some private interests of MPs, in total more bills than would be necessary to signal party positions might be introduced.

2.4 Conclusion

In this chapter, a formal model of oppositional bill introduction has been developed. Bills introduction is modeled to reflect strategic signaling of parties' policy positions. An analysis of the patterns of bill introduction over three or four policy dimensions in Belgium, France, Germany, and the United Kingdom reveals mixed evidence for the theoretical model. Clear evidence is found for the central empirical implication of the model that parties introduce more bills on a policy dimension on which they have a more central position. The hypothesized effect of the relative position of the status quo or the distance of an actor to the status quo could not be confirmed.

For the (non-policy) costs related with bill introduction the expected patterns could be found. Parties introduce more bills on salient policy dimensions and they sponsor more bills the larger the seat share of the party group. However, in France the effect of salience, and in Germany the effect of seat share cannot be found. This could be evidence for systematic differences in bill introduction between parliamentary democracies. In all countries but Germany more MPs of a party mean significantly more bills. The substantial size of this effect could be evidence that the number of MPs does not only lead to more bills because it reduces the relative costs of bill introduction, but also that there are incentives for individual MPs to be more active in legislation than justified by considerations of signaling policy positions. The lack of a significant effect of salience could be further evidence for some other motivation than a partisan logic driving at least parts of bill introduction. Chapter 4 will take up the evidence that – depending on the possibilities of MPs and the electoral incentives – bills could also serve as a means to pursue a personal vote.

Overall, there is substantial evidence to further investigate the vote-seeking explanation of bill introduction. Vote-seeking should not only take place through the signaling of the position of the party's policy program. In order to seek votes, parties should be especially aware of dealing with issues that are important to their voters. Evidence for vote-seeking on "most important problems" and differences in oppositional and governmental strategies will be dealt with in the next chapter.

2.5 Appendix to Chapter 2

Table 6 Summary Statistics of the Dependent and Independent Variables

Belgium (Walloon Parties)

Variable	Mean	Std. Dev.	Min	Max
Number of Bills per Actor, Policy Dimension, and Legislative Period	29.578	41.071	0	181
Distance of Actor to Median	3.185	3.163	0	13.962
Distance of Status Quo to Median	1.911	1.293	0.109	4.650
Distance of Actor to Status Quo	3.519	3.084	0.021	13.490
Salience of Policy Dimension	12.857	3.495	5	24.031
Seat Share	0.111	0.091	0.005	0.327
Maximal Distance in Coalition	4.644	4.593	0.331	15.789
Government	0.156	0.365	0	1
Parliamentary Majority	0.344	0.477	0	1
Opposition	0.5	0.502	0	1
Economic Dimension	0.25	0.435	0	1
Social Dimension	0.25	0.435	0	1
Environmental Dimension	0.25	0.435	0	1
Decentralization Dimension	0.25	0.435	0	1

Note: N = 128; the seat share variable enters the regression in logarithmic form.

Belgium (Flemish Parties)

Variable	Mean	Std. Dev.	Min	Max
Number of Bills per Actor, Policy Dimension, and Legislative Period	31.318	38.915	0	181
Distance of Actor to Median	2.775	2.993	0	12.2
Distance of Status Quo to Median	2.114	2.216	0.001	9.218
Distance of Actor to Status Quo	3.319	2.958	0.001	11.818

Salience of Policy Dimension	12.983	3.297	1	20
Seat Share	0.137	0.102	0.007	0.429
Maximal Distance in Coalition	4.538	3.888	0.278	14
Government	0.152	0.360	0	1
Parliamentary Majority	0.364	0.483	0	1
Opposition	0.484	0.502	0	1
Economic Dimension	0.25	0.435	0	1
Social Dimension	0.25	0.435	0	1
Environmental Dimension	0.25	0.435	0	1
Decentralization Dimension	0.25	0.435	0	1

Note: N = 132; the seat share variable enters the regression in logarithmic form.

France

Variable	Mean	Std. Dev.	Min	Max
Number of Bills per Actor, Policy Dimension, and Legislative Period	60.917	73.743	0	350
Distance of Actor to Median	3.489	3.907	0	15.465
Distance of Status Quo to Median	6.416	2.283	2.541	9.953
Distance of Actor to Status Quo	5.952	4.078	0	17.007
Salience of Policy Dimension	12.481	3.317	5.658	18.662
Seat Share	0.255	0.209	0.002	0.818
Maximal Distance in Coalition	2.668	2.895	0	8.275
Government	0.167	0.375	0	1
Parliamentary Majority	0.333	0.475	0	1
Opposition	0.5	0.504	0	1
Economic Dimension	0.333	0.475	0	1

Social Dimension	0.333	0.475	0	1
Environmental Dimension	0.333	0.475	0	1

Note: N = 72; the seat share variable enters the regression in logarithmic form.

Germany

Variable	Mean	Std. Dev.	Min	Max
Number of Bills per Actor, Policy Dimension, and Legislative Period	31.724	26.506	1	128
Distance of Actor to Median	4.069	3.696	0	15.628
Distance of Status Quo to Median	2.485	1.913	0.033	7.483
Distance of Actor to Status Quo	4.481	4.025	0.001	17.958
Salience of Policy Dimension	13.822	2.249	8.192	20.318
Seat Share	0.372	0.209	0.012	0.601
Maximal Distance in Coalition	4.604	3.487	0.157	10.727
Government	0.241	0.430	0	1
Parliamentary Majority	0.241	0.430	0	1
Opposition	0.518	0.503	0	1
Economic Dimension	0.333	0.474	0	1
Social Dimension	0.333	0.474	0	1
Environmental Dimension	0.333	0.474	0	1

Note: N = 87; the seat share variable enters the regression in logarithmic form.

United Kingdom

Variable	Mean	Std. Dev.	Min	Max
Number of Bills per Actor, Policy Dimension, and Legislative Period	20.604	28.104	0	119
Distance of Actor to Median	5.379	4.370	0	17.138
Distance of Status Quo to Median	3.040	2.228	0.021	7.762
Distance of Actor to Status Quo	5.961	4.155	0.021	16.639
Salience of Policy Dimension	12.749	2.758	6.557	17.954
Seat Share	0.260	0.260	0.005	0.636
Government	0.167	0.375	0	1
Parliamentary Majority	0.167	0.375	0	1
Opposition	0.666	0.474	0	1
Economic Dimension	0.25	0.435	0	1
Social Dimension	0.25	0.435	0	1
Environmental Dimension	0.25	0.435	0	1
Decentralization Dimension	0.25	0.435	0	1

Note: N = 96; the seat share variable enters the regression in logarithmic form.

3 Public Opinion and Parliamentary Activities

"Every law the people has not ratified in person is null and void – is, in fact, not a law." (Rousseau 1762, III: 15). Rousseau's statement, extreme as it may be by actually describing "representative democracy" as an oxymoron, points to an important normative minimal condition of representative democracies: Somehow the "will of the people" has to be represented in law-making.

Legislation is the most important means for the "authoritative allocation of values" (Easton 1953). In most modern democracies the formulation and implementation of laws lies in the hands of elected representatives. In a long-term perspective, elections in representative democracies have the function of connecting citizens' preferences and lawmakers' policy output. In parliamentary democracies the connection between preferences and output takes the following form: Parties offer certain policy choices, voters vote according to their preferences, the votes are translated into parliamentary seats. Those parliamentary seats constitute the basis for government formation, which is essential for the policy output. The policy output or the resulting policy outcomes can then be taken into account by utility-maximizing voters who prepare their next electoral choice. In line with this view on representation the model presented in the previous chapter understood bills as a way to signal policy positions not only during electoral campaigns but continuously between elections.

However, legislative activities may not only be programmatic signals of parties to voters. Due to time and budget constraints political actors cannot realize the entire set of their electoral promises, even if they command the parliamentary majority and intend to fulfill their promises. Therefore it is just as important for voters to know about the *salience* political actors attach to policy as it is to know the actors' policy positions (compare Laver 2001 for a discussion of the concepts of position and salience in the policies of political actors). Political actors can use bill sponsorship, and also other parliamentary activities, to signal salience. In a short-term perspective of representation, bill sponsorship can serve as a tool to respond immediately to changes in the public's priorities. Putting issues the voters care about on the parliamentary agenda is thus desirable from a normative standpoint. But also rational calculations could make parties react to public opinion in deciding which issues when to tackle, if parties expect that voters reward congruence between the public and the parliamentary agenda.

In this chapter, I will examine the responsiveness of political actors in their parliamentary activities to public opinion. The following three questions will be addressed: First, is there responsiveness to public opinion in parliamentary activities? Second, how does the status of being in government or opposition influence parliamentary responsiveness? And third, does the closeness of elections have an influence on the responsiveness to public concerns?

Unlike many other studies (see, e.g., Huber and Powell 1994 or Blais and Bodet 2006), I will not look at the congruence between positions of voters and their representatives. Instead, this chapter will examine the responsiveness of political actors to public opinion in their actual parliamentary activities in order to answer the question whether those political actors set the legislative agenda according to the priorities of the public. Another innovation of the analysis in this chapter is that it allows identifying time effects in the reaction of political actors to public opinion.

I will distinguish between three political actors when analyzing the responsiveness to public opinion: government, government parties, and opposition. From a normative perspective responsiveness of all actors is desirable. However, I anticipate differences due to a number of factors. For instance, whereas the government is expected to solve problems that arise and usually has the legislative majorities needed to implement policy changes, the opposition has more freedom in its reaction yet no majorities. The opposition acts as critics of government (non)reaction or as idea-givers, but their policy suggestions most of the time do not have any direct consequences. Differences in responsiveness of government and opposition to public opinion can also be expected with regard to the timing of responsiveness or concerning the question whether to respond at all.

The empirical part of this chapter examines the reactions of government, government parties, and opposition to public opinion in Germany. The case of Germany is well suited to examine the reaction of political actors to the opinion of the general public on a higher level of aggregation. The electoral system does not provide the same incentives for personal vote-seeking as do, for example, the electoral systems of the United Kingdom and France.[56] Even more importantly, many parliamentary activities that allow MPs to set the parliamentary agenda, such as bill sponsorship or interpellations, are collective activities in the German Bundestag, as they require the support of a party group or of at least five percent of the MPs. For these reasons it is likely that if parliamentary activities reflect public opinion, they will reflect the public opinion of the general public and not particularistic interests of a smaller geographic constituency. Also data availability makes the German case a good choice: There is a long monthly time series of

[56] This is at least true for the German MPs who were elected over the party lists.

survey data available on what the respondents perceive as the "most important problem" facing their country, as well as data on parliamentary activities for the same period.

The chapter is structured as follows: In the next section, I will review the relevant literature and introduce the main theoretical aspects of responsiveness and parliamentary activities. Then I derive three hypotheses, which I will test empirically after describing the data and the method of analysis used. The discussion of the results is followed by the conclusion.

3.1 Public Opinion, Parliamentary Activities, and Responsiveness

The principle of popular sovereignty is not only found in the writings of Rousseau. It is also reflected in Abraham Lincoln's famous description of the United States' democratic model as "government of the people, by the people, for the people" or, for example, in the first sentence of article 20, paragraph 3 of the Universal Declaration of Human Rights: "The will of the people shall be the basis of the authority of government." From a normative perspective it is unquestionable that the will of the people shall be represented by government. By which mechanisms the will of the people finds its way into policy-making is a question of institutional design of democracies. Ratification of laws by the people in person, as demanded by Rousseau, is an exception in modern democracies. Usually, the voters' participation in the government of their country is indirect, that is, through elected representatives.

The study of democracy has seen a long-standing debate on how representatives should fulfill their duty of representing. The most frequently used distinction is between trustee and delegate. A trustee, in the tradition of Edmund Burke's famous speech to the electors of Bristol in 1774 (Bromwich 2000: 55), is a representative who – once elected – acts autonomously according to his own judgment and conscience. A delegate, on the other hand, acts according to the preferences and instructions of his or her constituency. In modern parliamentary democracies the delegate model seems outdated and would even contradict the provisions of the constitution in many countries: The German Basic Law, for example, states explicitly in paragraph 1 of Article 38 that MPs "shall be representatives of the whole people, not bound by orders or instructions, and responsible only to their conscience." Similarly, paragraph 1 of Article 27 of the French Constitution declares: "No Member shall be elected with any binding mandate." Article 42 of the Belgian Constitution follows the same principle: "The members of the two Houses represent the Nation, and not only those who elected them."

Nonetheless, the outmodedness of the delegate model of representation does not imply that representatives necessarily follow a trustee model. Even if they do not take instructions from their constituencies, representatives often take instructions on how to vote from their parties. This is reflected in the high levels of party discipline usually observed in parliamentary democracies. A study (Wessels 2004) on members of the German Bundestag in 2003 reveals that German MPs see themselves as trustees rather than as delegates, but the results of the study also show the importance of the party factor. Asked how MPs should vote in case of conflict between their own opinion and the constituency voters' opinion, over 93 percent of the respondents[57] agreed that MPs should follow their own opinion. In a conflict between party opinion and constituency opinion, more than 67 percent stated that an MP should vote according to the party line.[58] Finally, in a conflict between party line and an MP's opinion, almost 60 percent of the responding MPs thought that one's own opinion should be the guideline for a voting decision.

Even if the majority of MPs maintained that, in case of a conflict, they would rather follow their own opinion or the party line instead of their constituency, this does not necessarily mean that voters' preferences do not play a role in an MP's parliamentary behavior. An MP's individual political opinion, as well as the party line, can be directly or indirectly influenced by the opinion of the public, in that political actors seek to win votes. Downs' (1957) economic model of democracy produces promising equilibrium results from a normative point of view: Policy outcomes are predicted to be located at the center of the voter distribution in a one-dimensional policy space when two vote-seeking parties or candidates compete against each other. Grofman (2004) shows that the convergence of policy positions depends on a dozen assumptions. But even if these assumptions are not usually met in parliamentary democracies, elections can still be seen as a tool to connect voter preferences and actions of their representatives. Powell (2000), for instance, distinguishes between a majoritarian and a proportional vision of democracy and reassesses the normative claim of the representative function of elections. He argues that the responsiveness of government formation to the citizens' votes and the representational congruence, that is, the question in how far the positions of the voters are reflected in the policies adopted, indicate the quality of representation through the electoral system. While government formation is more responsive to electoral outcomes in the majoritarian vision, electoral systems following the proportional vision of democracy reflect the median voters' position better.

57 The response rate was 34 percent.

58 Conflict of constituency and party position and the representation of constituency interests by individual MPs will be the focus of Chapter 4.

Responsiveness to sanctions in the form of elections (Rehfeld 2009) is likely to correspond to the responsiveness of political actors to the voters' interests. The latter form of responsiveness is in line with Pitkin (1967: 209), who sees responsiveness as a component of representation ("representing here means acting in the interest of the represented, in a manner responsive to them"). Eulau and Karps (1977: 62) distinguish between four forms of responsiveness: policy responsiveness, service responsiveness, allocation responsiveness, and symbolic responsiveness. As can be seen from these various usages of the term "responsiveness", there is no clear-cut definition of what responsiveness means. Parliamentary reactions can be purely symbolic or actually result in policy changes. Such "policy responsiveness" can be expected particularly from government or its parliamentary majority. Opposition parties, in turn, can support "policy responsiveness" by keeping an unsolved "important problem" on the agenda. Correspondingly, government and its support parties can also follow a "symbolic" strategy that does not really confront the problem at hand. I use the term as pertaining to the responsiveness of MPs, parties, or government to voters' opinion concerning the importance of policy issues. Parliamentary activities are understood as responsive as long as they put issues on the parliamentary agenda that the public thinks are important. The analysis is therefore restricted to responsiveness as regards the salience of policies. The research design adopted here does not allow to identify whether the parliamentary activities signal a certain policy position, and if they do, whether this position is in line with the majority opinion.

In modern representative democracies parties play an important role in the connection between voters' preferences and policy output. Parties with different policy positions and priorities compete for votes in elections. For the representation to work, the policies and priorities promised during the electoral campaign have to be reflected in the policies actually adopted, or at least attempted, by the elected representatives.

For government a number of studies suggest that legislation indeed reflects party positions as formulated in party manifestos. Legislation is the most important means to change policies and, hence, to fulfill electoral promises. Pomper (1968) analyzes the fulfillment of pledges that Democrats and Republicans in the United States made in their election platforms between 1944 and 1966. He finds that only around ten percent of the pledges are completely ignored. Depending on the measurement, between 50 percent and 75 percent of the promises are actually fulfilled. There is variance between parties and issues. Generally, the party of the president has a higher rate of keeping their pledges. Rose (1980) makes a similar check for Labour and Conservatives in the United Kingdom. His findings likewise show that campaign promises are generally kept by governments. Hofferbert and Klingemann (1990) and Klingemann et al. (1994) examine the congruence between, on the one hand, policy priorities in parties' election programs and, on the other hand, the priorities in government declarations as well as actual policy outcomes. Their findings show that election programs indeed contain information on what parties will do once they are in power, notwithstanding common prejudices regarding broken electoral promises. For Germany, Rölle (2000) analyzes the realization of party manifestos for the period 1949-1987 with regard to welfare state issues. He concludes with a "surprising résumé", namely that parties do as promised.[59] Pétry and Collette (2009) review 18 English and French articles analyzing this connection. Overall most of the studies show that parties actually implement a large proportion of their electoral promises once in government. These approaches, however, exclude oppositional legislative activities.

Chapter 2 of this study followed a similar line of argument, extended it to opposition, and offered a model that reflects the choice of issues actually dealt with. Against this background, bills are thought to reflect a party's programmatic positions and to signal these positions to the voters. Party priorities, however, are not translated directly into a legislative agenda, as parties, in order to win votes, rather decide strategically which issues to give priority. This does not contradict the findings of congruence between policy priorities in party programs and actual government priorities, however. The strategic considerations might even be able to explain some of the unexplained variance.

While there are good reasons to think that bills and also other parliamentary activities are reflections of party positions and priorities, this is certainly not the whole story. Pomper (1968: 200) sees two connections between programmatic issues and elections. On the one hand, party leaders and candidates have their own programmatic objectives and look for public endorsement by winning elections. On the other hand, there is indirect popular influence on political activities when politicians respond to popular demands or anticipate it in order to attract votes. Rose (1980), too, acknowledges alternative sources of government legislation or directives other than inspiration in election manifestos: In the 1970s, almost 90 percent of the government legislation in the United Kingdom had their origin in unexpected events or ongoing policy processes in the ministries (Rose 1980: 72).

59 However, the most "surprising" fact about Rölle's study is how he arrives at this conclusion given the data. He compares the percentage of welfare state issues in the party manifestos according to the CMP data with the percentage of each party's parliamentary activities concerning welfare state issues. He does not consider the direction of neither statements nor activities. He finds that the percentage of statements differs quite considerably between parties but the percentage of activities on welfare state issues does not differ a lot.

More recent literature focuses on these alternative sources of policy change other than programmatic positions of actors and electoral results. For the United States Baumgartner and Jones (1993) and Jones and Baumgartner (2005) suggest a dynamic perspective of policy change that considers the scarcity of attention, the role of information and events, as well as the need to take priorities in setting the policy agenda. Literature on policy agendas differs from classical studies on representation in that the focus is not on positions of actors but on priorities of issues. This approach has been applied to several other countries in the framework of the comparative agendas project (compare Baumgartner et al. 2011). The finding of "stickiness"[60] of policies in the US context (Jones and Baumgartner 2005) is also confirmed in a comparative perspective (Baumgartner et al. 2009). They conclude that policy change follows a "punctuated equilibrium"[61] rather than shifting directly with changing policy preferences of government. Jennings et al. (2011) point to the importance of "government core functions", which always range high on the government agenda. Finally, Jones et al. (2009) argue that public priorities are better represented in the early stages of policy agenda-setting, such as executive speeches, than in later stages, such as laws or budgets.

Jones et al. (2009) also look at actual legislative activities instead of just programmatic documents (as do, e.g., Adams et al. 2009), speeches, or policy outcomes (as do, e.g., Hobolt and Klemmensen 2008, Breeman et al. 2009). In this chapter, I will also focus on policy priorities rather than on positions as a measure of responsiveness and I will also examine actual parliamentary activities. One big advantage of this approach is that data on parliamentary activities is available on a high frequency basis, whereas new election manifestos are only produced every few years. In order to answer the research questions of this chapter some extensions to the dominant approach are needed: Instead of focusing either on government priorities or on the aggregate activities of the legislature, I will distinguish between activities of government, government parties, and parliamentary opposition. Additionally, I will analyze the data in a way that allows controlling for mutual influence between the actors as well as for effects over time.

---

60 "Stickiness" of policies implies that information is not directly translated into policy output. Costs imposed by cognitive "stickiness" of decision makers or "stickiness" of institutions get in the way of a direct translation (Jones and Baumgartner 2005: 158).

61 The punctuated equilibrium is a theory in evolutionary biology that claims that in the evolutionary change of species there are long phases of stagnation as well as phases of rapid change (Gould and Eldredge 1993). Baumgartner and Jones (1993) first applied this theory to policy change by arguing that long phases of policy stability are punctuated by rapid shifts in policy.

Studies of responsiveness that distinguish between different political actors and take actual parliamentary activities into account are rare. An exception is Brettschneider (1995), who examines the congruence between parliamentary activities and the majority opinion as well as the direction of opinion change. Brettschneider uses a very extensive data set, including all parliamentary activities from the first to the eleventh legislative period of the German Bundestag. However, the statistical analysis stays at a basic level. The author does not make use of the information he has on the timing of the bills and other forms of parliamentary activities.[62] His findings show that parliamentary questions are less responsive to voters' concerns than are bills, and therefore he assumes that parliamentary questions are more focused toward the constituency than toward the public as a whole. However, equally likely is that parliamentary activities do not always transport a certain policy position but rather point to a problem and put it on the parliamentary agenda to force government to consider the issue. The policy agendas approach of looking at priorities of issues is better suited to find responsive behavior in this case. Green-Pedersen and Mortensen (2010) consider influences of the opposition agenda (measured through issue priorities in parliamentary questions) on the party agenda (measured through issue priorities in parliamentary debates) and on the government agenda (measured through the analysis of executive speeches) in Denmark. However, the authors are not interested in the influence of public opinion on the issue priorities of either government or opposition. Using a similar approach, but with weekly instead of yearly data, Vliegenthart et al. (2011) look at inter-party agenda-setting in the Belgian parliament. Following these authors, I will focus on the parliamentary activities of diverse political actors. Like Green-Pedersen and Mortensen (2010) and Vliegenthart et al. (2011) I will concentrate on priorities instead of positions and like Brettschneider (1995) I will relate these priorities to public opinion.

3.2 Theoretical Expectations on Responsiveness to Public Opinion

Democracy as the rule of the people necessarily has to take public opinion into account or, as Key (1961: 7) puts it: "Unless mass views have some place in the shaping of policy, all the talk about democracy is nonsense." Hence, one can formulate a very general expectation that parties are responsive to public opinion. However, for instrumentally rational parties responsiveness is not for the sake of the democratic spirit, but to maximize votes. Parties, which follow an

---

62 Brettschneider does not have enough observations over time, because he uses survey data on positions on specific issues that were only asked infrequently.

instrumental logic, will therefore employ their reactions to public opinion strategically. Elections, in which parties compete for votes with alternative positions and priorities can thus connect policy generation and voter preferences. As laid out in the previous chapter, bill submission can be used for signaling programmatic positions through parliamentary activities. In addition to this long-term responsiveness to public opinion, parties can also respond to short-term shifts in public opinion in order to maximize their votes at the next elections or their levels of support in current public opinion surveys. These short-term reactions could be reflected in responsiveness through positional changes or through changes of priorities. In this chapter, I focus on the latter.

Programmatic positions as laid out in the election manifestos are certainly one viable source for parliamentary activities. Yet, time constraints might not allow political actors to become active on all issues considered in the manifesto. And even if setting priorities were not necessary, the party manifesto does not necessarily imply *when* to treat which issue. In addition, external "shocks" might generate legislative demands not foreseen at the time when the party manifesto is drafted or might lead to a revision of old positions or priorities. One important source in deciding which issues to consider at which point in time or which new issues to deal with should be public opinion. If voters are aware of an issue and deem it important, position-taking makes more sense for a party than in a case where voters are not interested in the issue.[63] Parliamentary activities do not necessarily have to signal positions, they could also be used to signal to the voters that their concerns are taken seriously and that the issues the voters care about are dealt with. From the considerations made above, the first hypothesis can be derived.

> *Hypothesis 1* The more important an issue for the public, the more likely that political actors put the issue on the political agenda.

Even if responsiveness to public opinion were worthwhile for all political actors from a vote-seeking as well as from a normative perspective, the degree to which political actors actually respond to public opinion should differ according to their government status, as the wish to react in a responsive manner might not concur with the possibilities to do so. I assume that there are different costs associated with being responsive depending on the status of the actor. First of all, all parliamentary parties have means at hand that are not very time-consuming and

[63] This is true for parties that want to send public signals of their positions or that want to show that they have the issues the voters care about on their agenda. A government that has to enforce unpopular cuts in social benefits might as well become active when the public attention to the issue is low.

consequently make responsive behavior quite easy. Asking oral or written questions, for instance, does not require much preparation compared to the drafting of a bill that is “coalition-”, “Bundesrat-”, and “constitutional court-proof”. This leads to the expectation that parliamentary parties, no matter whether they constitute the parliamentary majority or are in opposition, are more responsive than government.[64] Yet, there should also be differences among the parliamentary parties. Opposition parties are not bound by coalition agreements and do not need to coordinate with coalition partners or with the government’s agenda. They can criticize government activities freely. Additionally, their proposals are unlikely to be accepted, hence they can come forward with ideas that might not be fully developed yet. Alternatively, opposition can put “difficult” issues on the agenda by asking government to find a solution.

Government parties are more restrained in this respect. They can be expected to avoid proposing unpopular solutions at high levels of public attention and to rather delay issues. Also individual activities such as asking questions should be used to a lesser degree by government MPs than by the opposition, as the former have to fear measures of party discipline if they give the impression of criticizing government policies. Government activities, finally, need the most preparation and coordination, consequently I expect government to be the least responsive of the three actors, opposition parties, government parties, and government.

Hypothesis 2 Opposition parties react faster and more pronounced to public opinion than do government parties. Governments respond the slowest and weakest.

If political actors are responsive to public opinion out of vote-seeking motivation, one should see a connection between elections and responsiveness. Nordhaus (1975: 182) assumes that voters have a waning memory of past (economic) events. Empirical research on economic voting has confirmed that voters take especially the economic conditions shortly before elections into account when making their voting decision (e.g. Alesina et al. 1993, Lewis-Beck and Stegmaier 2000). On the same token research on political knowledge suggests that the voters’ level of information and political knowledge is the highest in the year before elections (Andersen et al. 2005). Consequently, political parties’ attention to public opinion should be especially pronounced when elections are

[64] This expectation is of course partly connected to the operationalization of parliamentary activities. Governments also have possibilities to respond quickly, for instance with press releases or interviews.

close, as the payoff for being responsive should be the highest then. This should apply to opposition but also to government party and cabinet activities[65] and leads to the third hypothesis:

> *Hypothesis 3* Political actors are more responsive to public opinion when elections are close.

In the following, I will describe the data and method used to test these hypotheses empirically.

3.3 Empirical Evidence from the German Bundestag

3.3.1 Data and Measurements

In this chapter, I attempt to test whether and how government, government parties, and opposition respond in their parliamentary activities to the public's perception of the "most important problem" facing a country. The empirical part uses time series data on parliamentary activities and public opinion in Germany. The focal independent variable "public opinion" is operationalized using the "most important problem"-question of the "Politbarometer"-surveys.[66] The data is available on a monthly basis since May 1989. In the following, I analyze data up to the Bundestag elections in 2005 (consequently, the observation period includes parts of the 11th legislative period and the entire 12th through 15th legislative periods).[67] The "most important problem"-question captures the priorities the public attaches to a number of topics. Every respondent is asked to state

---

65 For government and governing parties another effect might add to higher levels of responsiveness: The declining spoils of being in office as the next election comes closer might not only lead to an increased probability of government termination (Lupia and Strøm 1995) but also to less consideration of the views of coalition partners. This provides better opportunities for governing parties to be responsive without being restraint by mutual consideration of the coalition partners' positions.

66 The Politbarometer-survey is conducted by the Forschungsgruppe Wahlen, Mannheim. The data is accessible at the GESIS Data Archive for the Social Sciences (ZA-Nr. 2391).

67 In seven years during this 16-year period the survey has not been taken during the month of July. To make up for this gap in the data, I assume that without new information politicians will rely on past information in taking their decision on which issues to focus. Hence, I fill in the gap using the data of the previous month.

which problems facing Germany he or she deems the most important and which the second most important.[68]

During the period under discussion the "most important problem"-question contains overall 106 categories in which the answers of the respondents are coded. Often the answers deal with very short-lived issues, such as item 63 about the CDU secretary general Geißler, item 64 about Gorbachev's visit to Germany, or item 103 concerning the tsunami in the Indian Ocean in December 2004. A majority of the categories have only been used for one or a few months and are therefore not suited for a dynamic analysis of political reactions to public opinion.[69] Other categories have to be excluded from the analysis because they refer to very wide or multiple problems. For these categories it is hardly possible to identify political reactions falling into the same category, which could therefore be caused by public concerns.[70] Another problem excludes more items from analysis: Even though a considerable number of the remaining items have a concise subject area and have been answer categories over a long time period, some of them have never exceeded very low levels of attention. Item 37 "conflict in the Middle East" as well as item 65 "shop closing time" were mentioned over several years respectively, but even at their peaks only 1.1 percent of the respondents perceived those items among the most important problems facing Germany.

The categories used for the empirical analyses in this chapter are "unemployment", "foreigners", "pensions", "right-wing extremism", and "BSE". The selection is based on the following criteria: The categories are precise enough to identify parliamentary activities that clearly relate to the topic mentioned by the respondents, they have been a concern for the respondents for more than one year, and they are a concern for at least 30 percent of the population at one point in time. The first selected issue is "unemployment", the topic that receives most

---

68 The question, which has not changed between 1989 and 2005, is formulated as follows: "Was ist Ihrer Meinung nach gegenwärtig das wichtigste Problem in Deutschland? Und was ist ein weiteres wichtiges Problem?" ("What is the most important problem in Germany at the moment, in your opinion? And what is another important problem?" – own translation; also the translations of items that follow below are my own translations of the German text).

69 54 of the 106 categories have been used in less than a year between 1989 and 2005.

70 Examples are item 30 "other domestic policy issues", item 41 "general foreign policy issues", item 57 "other social problems", item 66 "other problems", and item 67 "other personal issues". But also item 2 "social policy, health policy, family policy", item 44 "problems in the former GDR/ reunification in general", or item 15 "environmental protection" are too general to assume a causal link between public opinion and policy reactions. For example, the public might be concerned about water protection, hence parliamentary activities concerned with air pollution would not be responsive. Unfortunately, the broad item "environment" does not allow to make more refined distinctions.

mentions as first or second most important problem in more than three quarters of the time during the period under observation. However, the issue also shows considerable variation: In January 1991, not even seven percent saw "unemployment" among the two most important problems, whereas more than 90 percent thought so in February 1998. Overall, in the 16 years studied here, on average over 55 percent of the respondents think that "unemployment" is a most important problem. This is by far the highest overall average among all issues mentioned by the respondents.

Far behind follow, in descending order, the issues "foreigners" (ten percent on average), "environment" (nine percent on average), "economic situation" (eight percent on average), and "pensions" (seven percent on average). The issues "environment" and "economic situation" have been excluded from the following analysis as the categories they represent are too broad. The category "foreigners" is sometimes coded together with the category "asylum seekers". In order to have the same categories over the whole period, I joint these two categories into one.[71] Taken together, "foreigners/asylum seekers", the second issue selected, is seen as a "most important problem" by almost 17 percent of the respondents on average. One of two items received a majority of mentions in 15 out of 197 months studied here.[72]

The third issue that I study, "pensions", is constantly perceived as a major problem by some, but never by a majority of the respondents during the length of this study. The same is true for item 58 "right-wing extremism", which follows on rank twelve with an average of four percent mentions. It has been selected as fourth issue as it is a narrow category allowing easy identification of related parliamentary activities.[73] The fifth issue that fulfills the selection criteria is the topic "BSE". For two months it was perceived as the most important problem by a majority of the respondents. The issue "BSE" differs from the other issues selected with respect to its relatively short duration on the public agenda. It represents a "shooting star" event that is perceived as very important at one point in time and is then forgotten more or less quickly. Its inclusion in the analysis allows some insights whether responsiveness in the case of "sudden" events differs from the dynamics observed for more "constant" problems.

Taken together, the five selected topics include the problem that received most mentions as one of the two most important problems in 166 out of 197

71 The categories "foreigners" and "asylum seekers" have been joint categories before May 1989 and again since April 2005. I use the two as joint categories during the whole period.

72 14 times "asylum seekers" and once "foreigners".

73 Next to the already mentioned categories, the following categories have high averages: "Other problems", "problems related to reunification", "disappointment by politics and parties/affairs/donations", "peace and order/crime", "taxation".

months.[74] The overall mentions of these five topics are at their lowest right after reunification (when the five topics comprise only seven percent of all issues mentioned) and at their highest level in January 2001 (when over 70 percent of issues mentioned are covered). The median value of mentions of "most important problems" accounted for by these five issues lies at almost 52 percent.

The data, combined with information on parliamentary activities by different actors, allows quantitative testing of the hypotheses formulated above. Information on parliamentary activities is available on the website of the Documentation and Information System for Parliamentary Materials (DIP)[75], which lists all kinds of parliamentary activities on the party level (such as legislative initiatives, minor and major interpellations, motions, or debates on matters of topical interest), as well as on the individual level (for instance, speeches, or oral or written questions). The information reaches back to December 1976 with the beginning of the 8th legislative period. Due to constraints concerning the availability of public opinion data the analysis provided in this chapter starts in the year 1989.[76]

For the construction of the dependent variables, information on all parliamentary activities available to government, to parliamentary party groups, and to individual MPs was retrieved. There are, on the one hand, activities that are potentially suited to regulate, to change policies, or to have direct fiscal consequences, and there are, on the other hand, activities that mainly have controlling or communicating functions. The first group consists of bills[77], ordinances, and general administrative regulations. The latter two instruments are exclusively in the hand of governments. The second group of activities is predominantly used by opposition parties: minor and major interpellations, motions, debates on matters of topical interest ("Aktuelle Stunde"), and activities in the hands of individual MPs, such as oral and written questions.[78] The government counterpart of these instruments is the use of government declarations ("Regierungserklärungen"), which can be used for communication purposes. Government

[74] The rest of the time the following issues received most mentions: GDR/reunification related issues (25x), environment (3x), Iraq (2x), and energy taxation (1x).

[75] http://dip.bundestag.de, accessed on 24 November 2011.

[76] Due to changes in the structure of the DIP online data base for the data of legislative periods after 2005, a further extension of the observation period was not possible within the framework of this study.

[77] Opposition bills, however, mainly have a communicating function.

[78] There are differences in the usage of instruments not only between parliamentary majority and opposition but also between different opposition parties. The odd one out is the PDS for being the only party that generally used the collective instrument "minor interpellation" (which requires the support of a parliamentary group or at least five percent of the MPs) more frequently than oral and written questions (which can be asked by individual MPs).

communications ("Unterrichtung durch die Bundesregierung") can play a similar role. According to Article 43 Paragraph 2 of the German Basic Law, the Federal Government has the right to be heard at all times.

In order to identify parliamentary activities on the five selected topics, I distinguished relevant keywords in the keyword list provided by the DIP-data base, checked the results for their relevance, and refined the keyword selection if necessary.[79] The data retrieved from the data base was processed with the help of Stata programming in order to identify the kind of parliamentary activity, the relevant actor, and the date of the activity. The data was then aggregated to determine the number of monthly activities per actor (government, parliamentary majority, and opposition). Table 12 through Table 16 in the Appendix to this chapter show the distribution of the different instruments over the selected issues for the different political actors.[80]

Visual inspection of, on the one hand, the data on the public perception of the importance of a problem and, on the other hand, parliamentary activities indicates that there is some connection between the two. 0 shows five separate time series graphs of the public opinion measure for each topic as well as the number of parliamentary activities. "Unemployment" is the topic that receives by far the most attention. This is not met, however, by comparable levels of attention on the part of the political actors, who are more active on issues such as "foreigners" and "pensions", even though the public is less concerned with these topics. At least since the Schröder government was elected in 1998, the general public's increasing concerns with unemployment has gone along with increasing levels of activities by the political actors, but for the other selected issues parallel movements can still be observed more easily.

---

79 The following keywords were used in order to identify the topics: "Arbeitslos$", "Ausländer 'o' Asylanten 'o' Aussiedler 'o' Asyl 'o' doppelte Staatsbürgerschaft 'o' Zuwanderung", "Rente$ 'o' Pension$ 'n' Pension (Unterkunft)", "rechtsextrem$ 'o' rechtsradikal$ 'o' fremdenfeindlich$ 'o' ausländerfeindlich$ 'o' Republikaner 'o' DVU 'o' NPD 'o' Antisemitismus", "BSE".

80 The tables report the frequency with which these instruments are used by government, parliamentary majority, and opposition. The activities of these actors will be analyzed in more detail in the remainder of this chapter. In addition, also "mixed" initiatives are reported where cooperation across the majority-opposition-divide takes place. Yet, as this cooperation is rather rare on most issues, it is not well suited for time series analyses. Case studies could help to find out more on the role of public opinion in influencing inter-party cooperation.

Figure 6 Public Opinion and Parliamentary Activities (1989-2005)

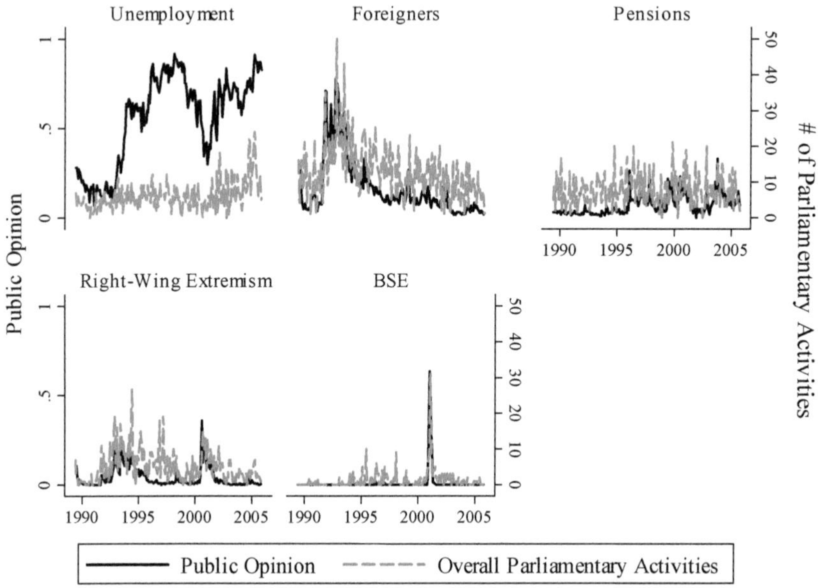

Source: Politbarometer (ZA-Nr. 2391), own calculations.

In order to grasp the relationship between these variables with some statistical foundation, I use regression techniques. In addition to the focal "public opinion" variable I include a dummy variable "election year", which takes the value 1 if an election takes place within the next twelve months and the value 0 otherwise. I also examine the interaction effect between the dummy variable and the public opinion measure to test whether political actors show different levels of responsiveness when taking the closeness of elections into account. Further, I consider past activities of other political actors to control for the possibility that they react on the activities of others (compare Vliegenthart et al. 2011 for inter-party agenda-setting in Belgium). Finally, I include a dummy to control for the different composition of government in the period studied. The "Kohl"-dummy takes the value 1 during the chancellorship of Helmut Kohl and his CDU/CSU, FDP coalition and the value 0 when Gerhard Schröder was chancellor of a coalition of Social Democrats and Greens.

3.3.2 Direction of Causal Effects

Before I come to the statistical analysis of the influence exerted by public opinion on parliamentary activities of opposition, government party groups, and government, I will test whether the empirical data supports the supposed causal direction, namely that public opinion influences parliamentary activities and not the other way around. A responsive government should react to the preferences of the public. It is also possible, however, that the activities of political actors influence public attention to certain problems.

One concept to test the causal direction in time series analysis is Granger causality (Granger 1969), which assumes that in time series regression causal effects can be identified. Past values of one variable can cause future values of other variables (and also future values of the variable itself). Using vector autoregressive models (VAR) one can model several dependent variables to depend on their own lags and lagged values of the other variables. Simple Wald tests allow to perform pairwise Granger causality tests to see whether the lags of one variable jointly Granger cause the other variable when controlling for its own lags. Granger causality tests as well as VAR models are widespread in economics but have also been applied in political science research (compare Freeman 1983 and Freeman et al. 1989 for early discussions, Sattler et al. 2008 or Toshkov 2011 for more recent applications, and Brandt and Sandler 2012 for the newest developments). Running VAR models with two lags[81] for the parliamentary activities of the different actors and for public opinion, separately for the different issues, and performing Granger causality tests shows that the main causal direction goes as expected from public opinion to parliamentary activities. The results of the Granger causality tests based on VAR(2) models are shown in Table 7.

For all topics the tests suggest a causal effect of past public opinion on the level of current activity of opposition parties. The same can be said about government parties' activities on the issues "foreigners", "BSE", and "right-wing extremism" and about cabinet activities on "foreigners" and "BSE". In addition to the causal direction from public opinion to activities, the reverse direction can likewise be established for opposition and government party activities concerning "BSE" and for government party activities on "right-wing extremism": These activities also influence public opinion.

81 The Bayesian information criterion (BIC) was used to find the optimal lag length for the VAR model. For all models the more parsimonious model with two lags was superior to models including three or four lags.

Table 7 Results of Granger Causality Tests for Activities and Public Opinion

Most important problem	Direction	χ^2	p-Value	Causal Relation
Opposition				
Unemployment	Opinion → Activity Activity → Opinion	10.498 1.861	0.005 0.394	Opinion influences activities
Foreigners	Opinion → Activity Activity → Opinion	26.793 0.119	0.000 0.942	Opinion influences activities
Pensions	Opinion → Activity Activity → Opinion	19.694 0.028	0.000 0.986	Opinion influences activities
Right-Wing Extremism	Opinion → Activity Activity → Opinion	18.648 4.212	0.000 0.122	Opinion influences activities
BSE	Opinion → Activity Activity → Opinion	331.530 11.297	0.000 0.004	Mutual influence
Government Parties				
Unemployment	Opinion → Activity Activity → Opinion	1.326 1.262	0.515 0.532	No causal relation
Foreigners	Opinion → Activity Activity → Opinion	26.931 4.195	0.000 0.123	Opinion influences activities
Pensions	Opinion → Activity Activity → Opinion	2.228 2.364	0.328 0.307	No causal relation
Right-Wing Extremism	Opinion → Activity Activity → Opinion	12.842 13.103	0.002 0.001	Mutual influence
BSE	Opinion → Activity Activity → Opinion	139.370 13.958	0.000 0.001	Mutual influence
Government				
Unemployment	Opinion → Activity Activity → Opinion	2.299 0.678	0.317 0.713	No causal relation
Foreigners	Opinion → Activity Activity → Opinion	7.033 0.329	0.030 0.848	Opinion influences activities
Pensions	Opinion → Activity Activity → Opinion	3.579 4.598	0.167 0.100	No causal relation

Right-Wing Extremism	Opinion → Activity Activity → Opinion	1.224 0.360	0.542 0.835	No causal relation
BSE	Opinion → Activity Activity → Opinion	14.222 3.943	0.001 0.139	Opinion influences activities

Note: The causal relation stated in the last column is statistically significant at the five percent level. The Granger causality tests are based on VAR(2) models with 195 observations each.

One could imagine other causal effects: Next to public opinion causing parliamentary activities, or parliamentary activities causing changes in the level of people who perceive a topic as "most important problem", actual problem pressure could influence both the public's perception of the problem as well as parliamentary activities. At least for parliamentary activities also the reverse causal relationship can be imagined, namely, that parliamentary activities (especially government bills) influence for example the unemployment rate. Additionally, complex causal patterns could exist between political actors. One actor could respond with parliamentary activities to the activities of another actor. I test these potential additional causal mechanisms using a five-variable VAR model and Granger causality tests for the topic "unemployment", because this is the only topic where monthly problem-pressure data are available.

The results of the VAR(5) model allowing for two lags are presented in Table 8. The findings indicate that public opinion as well as the unemployment rate Granger cause parliamentary activities of opposition. Government activities also Granger cause oppositional activities: The more government has made use of parliamentary activities concerning unemployment in the past, the less active opposition is in the present on this issue. The unemployment rate also Granger causes the perception of unemployment as a major problem. The unemployment rate, however, is unaffected by either the parliamentary activities of political actors, or by the public perception of unemployment as the most important problem. Likewise, no causal effects could be established for any of the variables on the parliamentary activities of cabinet or government party groups.

Hence, the VAR(5) model shows that the actual unemployment rate influenced the parliamentary activities of opposition but did not eradicate the effect of public opinion. While the actual unemployment rate (not surprisingly) also influences the public perception of unemployment as "most important problem", there is still an independent effect of the perceived problem pressure on oppositional activities when controlling for actual problem pressure. Hence, even though the perceived problem pressure contains some of the actual problem pressure, it seems reasonable to assume that political actors actually react to both and that public opinion data contains additional valuable information for politicians who decide on their agenda.

Table 8 Mutual Dependence between Activities of Political Actors, Public Opinion, and Actual Problem Pressure for the Topic "Unemployment"

Direction	χ^2	p-Value	Causal Relation
Gov. Parties' Act. → Gov. Activities	0.883	0.643	
Opp. Activities → Gov. Activities	3.355	0.187	
Public Opinion → Gov. Activities	3.176	0.204	No causal relations
Unempl. Rate → Gov. Activities	0.307	0.858	
All → Gov. Activities	9.334	0.315	
Gov. Activities → Gov. Parties' Act.	1.879	0.391	
Opp. Activities → Gov. Parties' Act.	2.493	0.288	
Public Opinion → Gov. Parties' Act.	2.520	0.284	No causal relations
Unempl. Rate → Gov. Parties' Act.	1.364	0.506	
All → Gov. Parties' Act.	9.070	0.336	
Gov. Activities → Opp. Activities	7.716	0.021	Opposition activities influenced by past government activities (-) and by public opinion and unemployment rate (+)
Gov. Parties' Act. → Opp. Activities	3.537	0.171	
Public Opinion → Opp. Activities	11.254	0.004	
Unempl. Rate → Opp. Activities	14.929	0.001	
All → Opp. Activities	41.431	0.000	
Gov. Activities → Public Opinion	1.729	0.421	Public opinion driven by actual unemployment rate
Gov. Parties' Act. → Public Opinion	0.974	0.615	
Opp. Activities → Public Opinion	0.890	0.641	
Unempl. Rate → Public Opinion	14.174	0.001	
All → Public Opinion	17.987	0.021	
Gov. Activities → Unempl. Rate	0.931	0.628	No causal relations
Gov. Parties' Act. → Unempl. Rate	0.452	0.798	

Opp. Activities → Unempl. Rate	1.097	0.578
Public Opinion → Unempl. Rate	1.380	0.502
All → Unempl. Rate	3.469	0.902

Note: The causal relations stated in the last column are statistically significant at the five percent level. The Granger causality tests are based on a VAR(5) model with 195 observations.

Overall, the VAR models indicate that public opinion influences parliamentary activities at least for opposition parties. For the other parties the influence depends on the topic. The dependence structure between parliamentary activities of different political actors seems to be not a big problem.[82] Oppositional activities on some topics are Granger caused by past activities of other actors, but the causal direction seems to go only one way. Therefore it is justified to analyze the factors that cause the parliamentary behavior of the different groups in separate single equation models as done later.

Yet, the results of the VAR models should not be given too much weight. VAR models are not well suited for dependent variables with a count structure, as these multivariate models assume a linear relationship between the different dependent variables and their lags.

3.3.3 Time Series Count Regression Model

As outlined above, the dependent variable of interest is the aggregate number of parliamentary activities per month by a certain parliamentary actor. The dependent variable has a discrete count structure then. Likelihood ratio tests show that (almost) all models presented below suffer from overdispersion. This would make the negative binomial regression model well suited for the analysis of the data.

The time series structure of the data, however, potentially adds complications. The augmented Dickey-Fuller unit-root test as well as the Phillips-Perron unit-root test indicate that the dependent variables were produced by a stationary

82 For the other topics VAR(4) models without the problem pressure variable were applied. But as they add few interesting additional information, the results are not presented here. The findings on public opinion and activities are robust to the results reported. In addition the models show that government activities on the topics "unemployment" and "foreigners" Granger cause oppositional activities. Additionally, government parties' activities concerning "BSE" Granger cause oppositional activities as well.

process. Yet, the presence of serial correlation could invalidate the statistical inferences drawn from a simple static count regression model. Cameron and Trivedi (1998: 221) maintain that time series models of count data are still in their infancy. They present a number of models that have been developed but state that "it is not clear which, if any, of the current models will become the dominant model for time series count data" (Cameron and Trivedi 1998: 221).[83]

A simple test whether serial correlation is indeed present in the data is to check whether the current and lagged raw residuals of a count regression are correlated (Cameron and Trivedi 2001: 343). Alternatively, Cameron and Trivedi (1998: 288) suggest a Box-Pierce portmanteau test for standardized Pearson residuals. Running static negative binomial models and testing for serial correlations in the residuals gives the following results: Strongest evidence for serial correlation is found in the case of oppositional parliamentary activities as dependent variable. Only for the issue "pensions" there is no serial correlation in the residuals according to both tests. The test for raw residuals also does not find serial correlation in the residuals of the regression on oppositional activities concerning the issue "BSE". The problem of serial correlation in the residuals is less clear for government parties' parliamentary activities. In the raw residuals there is only serial correlation left for the issue "BSE". In the Pearson residuals serial correlation occurs for the issues "BSE", "unemployment", and "right-wing extremism". For the government's parliamentary activities no serial correlation is present in any Pearson residuals of the static count regressions. In the raw residuals of the regression of cabinet activities on the topic "right-wing extremism" serial correlation is detected.

A simple adjustment to the cross-sectional negative binomial regression model is to enter the lagged dependent variable in the conditional mean function (compare Cameron and Trevedi 2001: 344): $\mu_{it} = \exp(x_i\beta + \rho \ln(y_{it-1} + 0.5))$.[84] This autoregressive model deals reasonably well with the problem of serial correlation. The tests described above detect no more serial correlation in the residuals of the models presented in Table 9 through Table 11.[85] In addition to solving problems of serial correlation, the lagged dependent variable could also be interpreted on substantial terms, since, for instance, opposition questions asked today

83 Cameron repeated this claim in a lecture held at UCLA in 2009 (the slides of the lecture can be viewed on http://cameron.econ.ucdavis.edu/racd/trcountIII4up.pdf, accessed on 30 April 2011).

84 0.5 is added to the actual count of parliamentary activities to guarantee a non-zero lagged value of y.

85 Only in the residuals of the model on the cabinet's parliamentary activities on "right-wing extremism" some (negative) serial correlation is still present. This is likely to be caused by the relatively few government activities on this topic. Therefore one can expect that a month with activities on the issue is followed by a month without activities.

might lead to more questions tomorrow. For government activities the contrary could be true, as today's activities might solve the problem at hand and make tomorrow's activities unnecessary. The inclusion of the lagged dependent variable in the cases where no serial correlation is detected in the static models does not affect the substantial results. As a robustness check I also run log-linear regression models using a Poisson distribution and allowing for autocorrelation and overdispersion (Aurelio and Campbell 1998).[86] In this model, instead of the lagged dependent variable, the lagged residuals are entered.[87] The results are presented in the Appendix to this chapter.[88]

3.3.4 *Empirical Results*

The results for the different actors (opposition, government parties, and government) are presented in separate tables. Table 9 shows the negative binomial regression model that identifies factors influencing the opposition's parliamentary activities. The lagged dependent variable has a positive coefficient in all five models and is statistically significant in four of them. This implies that opposition parties are more likely to be active in parliament when they were already more active in the previous month. This is especially true for the topics "unemployment", "foreigners and asylum seekers", "right-wing extremism", and "BSE". The next two variables test the influence of the parliamentary activities of government parties or of the cabinet in the previous month. Only for the topics "unemployment" and "foreigners" a statistically significant effect is found: The

86 The model has been developed for medical statistics but has also been applied in a political science context before (Schneider and Ruoff 2010). For other time series event count models and applications in political science compare Brandt et al. (2000) and Brandt and Williams (2001).

87 For OLS regression there is a debate about the pros and cons of including the lagged dependent variable in the model (compare, e.g., Achen 2000 and Keele and Kelly 2006). The problem that the lagged dependent variable leads to a downward bias of the other independent variables could potentially also arise in count models, but the debate has not yet extended to count models and there are no rules of thumb available when such a model should not be used. Aurelio and Campbell (1998: 34) argue that problems of bias are unlikely in their model in which the lagged dependent variable enters the model implicitly. If this is true, the robustness of the results suggests that the problem is also minor in my models including the lagged dependent variable. Additionally, as the comparison of the models with lagged dependent variable and without lagged dependent variable shows, even though many coefficients of the independent variables are smaller and the standard errors often larger, the differences are not dramatic. Therefore the results presented above should suffer from no major downward bias of the coefficients.

88 Most results are robust over the different model specification. This is in line with the findings of Jung et al. (2005), who compare a larger number of different time series count models and find very similar estimation results across the different models.

more government did on these issues in the past, the fewer activities opposition parties subsequently show. If government, however, neglects these topics, opposition parties are more likely to take them up.

In non-election years the effect of public opinion on oppositional activities in parliament is positive and statistically significant for all issues. The more the public was concerned with the issue in the previous month, the more current activities opposition parties show. The interaction term between public opinion and the election year is positive for the issues "unemployment", "foreigners", "pensions", and "right-wing extremism". For the topic "BSE" the regressions for all actors were run without interaction, because only in three months during election years BSE was perceived as most important problem (by less than one percent of the population). The interaction term is only statistically significant for the activities concerning "unemployment". The election year dummy has a negative sign in all equations and is statistically significant for the topics "unemployment", "foreigners", and "right-wing extremism". This means that opposition parties are significantly less active on these issues in election years, if the issues are not perceived as one of the two major problems by the entire population. Obviously, for all models the overall effect of public opinion on parliamentary activities is positive in election years and in non-election years. However, it is not possible given the information in Table 9 alone to see whether there is a significant difference between the effect of public opinion in the year before an election and the effect during the rest of the electoral period. In order to grasp the effect of the variables election year and public opinion as well as of the interaction term more fully, I present the effect graphically.

Table 9 Negative Binomial Regression of Opposition's Parliamentary Activities

	Unemployment	Foreigners	Pensions	Right-Wing Extremism	BSE
Opp. Parl. Activities $^{X}_{(t-1)}$	0.233*** (0.06)	0.189*** (0.06)	0.038 (0.08)	0.449*** (0.06)	0.525*** (0.18)
Gov. Parties' Parl. Activities$_{(t-1)}$	-0.079 (0.05)	0.005 (0.02)	-0.006 (0.05)	-0.069 (0.05)	0.213 (0.24)
Government's Parl. Activities$_{(t-1)}$	-0.117** (0.05)	-0.057** (0.03)	-0.025 (0.02)	0.121 (0.08)	-0.165 (0.15)
Public Opinion$_{(t-1)}$	0.491** (0.24)	0.822** (0.35)	2.447*** (0.95)	2.911*** (0.76)	3.239*** (1.06)

Election X $PO_{(t-1)}$	0.940**	0.984	1.031	2.377	
	(0.44)	(0.82)	(2.09)	(2.08)	
Election Year	-0.511*	-0.304**	-0.279	-0.287*	-0.104
	(0.30)	(0.14)	(0.17)	(0.15)	(0.28)
Kohl (6/1989-10/1998)	-0.248**	0.053	-0.193	0.163	-0.101
	(0.10)	(0.09)	(0.12)	(0.10)	(0.26)
Constant	1.100***	1.753***	1.407***	0.668***	-0.434**
	(0.17)	(0.14)	(0.16)	(0.11)	(0.20)
Wald $\chi^2(7)$	86.40***	56.15***	33.31***	151.74***	112.47***
α	0.1581***	0.1749***	0.2283***	0.2593***	1.2614***
N	196	196	196	196	196

^{X} The lagged dependent variable enters the equation in the following form: $\ln(y_{it-1} + 0.5)$; * significant at 10 percent ** at 5 percent *** at 1 percent; robust standard errors in parentheses; Wald $\chi^2(6)$ for the "BSE" model without the interaction term.

Figure 7 shows the difference in the expected number of parliamentary activities of opposition in election and non-election years given a certain level of public opinion. All other variables were set to their median values.[89] The histogram at the bottom of each graph shows the distribution of public opinion measure. It can be seen that for very low levels of public attention to the problem "unemployment" (when fewer than nine percent deem it a most important problem) opposition parties would introduce fewer bills on average. This finding is statistically significant at the ten percent level. If all variables are held at their median we would expect on average around one activity less in election years than in years without federal elections for such low levels of public attention.

89 I adapted the Stata code by Brambor et al. (2006) for the negative binomial regression model to create these figures. Standard errors are derived using simulation techniques as described in Brambor et al. (2006).

Figure 7 Difference in Expected Number of Oppositional Activities in Election and non-Election Years

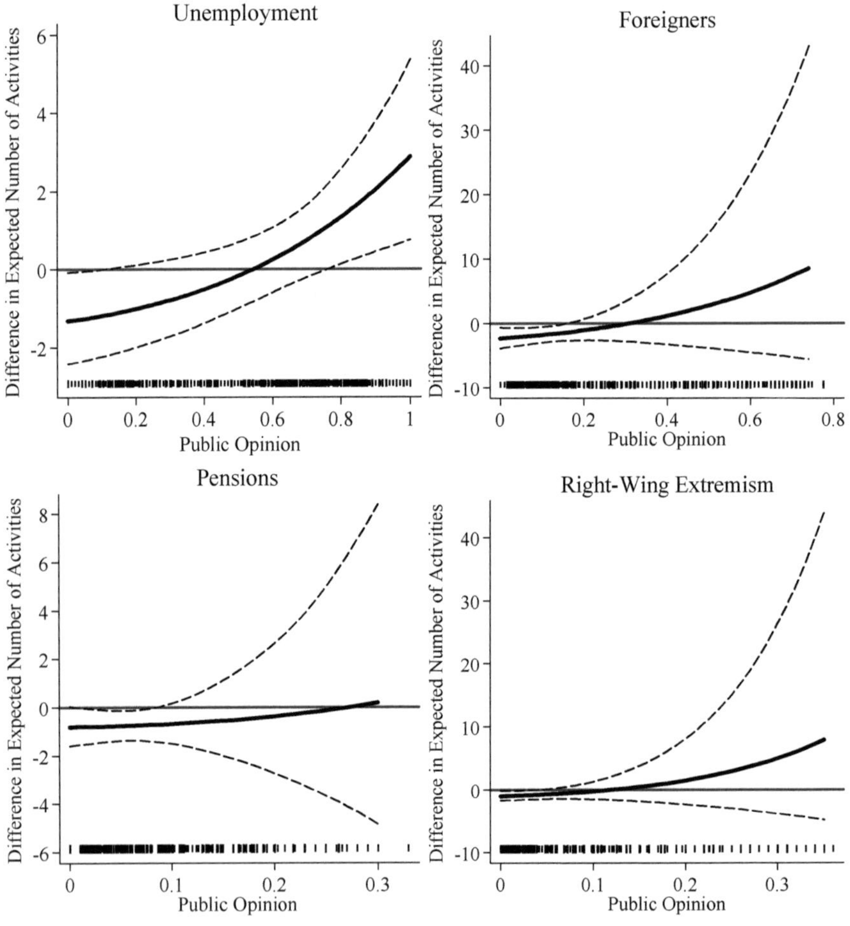

Note: Dashed line shows the 90 percent confidence interval; all other variables were set to their median values. The histogram at the bottom of each graph shows the distribution of the public opinion variable.

This situation is, however, almost out of the range of empirically observed values. Only in two months around the time of reunification fewer than nine percent of the population thought that "unemployment" did not belong to the two most important problems. The other extreme can be observed more often: If more than 76 percent of the population think that "unemployment" is among the two most important problems, opposition parties will be more active in election years than in non-election years. For the specification displayed here one would expect three additional activities on average in election years when all voters deem "unemployment" an important problem. In such a situation one would expect 5.5 activities in non-election years and 8.5 activities in election years, holding all other variables at their medians. Without public attention the expectation lies between three activities in non-election years and two activities on average in election years.

The graphical representation that illustrates the different effects of public opinion depending on whether the next Bundestag election takes place within the next twelve months looks similar for the other issues. All these issues have in common that there is only a statistically significant difference in the effect of public opinion between election years and non-election years at very low levels of public opinion. For the topic "foreigners" there is a significant difference in activities depending on the election year variable as long as fewer than 17 percent find the topic very relevant. This is the case in 70 percent of the time. In election years in which the topic does not play any role for the voters one would expect around 6.5 oppositional activities, in non-election years there would be on average nine activities. At higher levels of public attention the difference is much larger but not statistically significant (17 activities in non-election years and 27 activities in election years when 80 percent of the voters care a lot about this issue). For the topic "pensions" a statistically significant difference between election and non-election years is only observed when between one and eight percent of respondents think that the issue is one of the two most important problems. The substantial difference amounts to a difference of less than one activity on average. Similarly for "right-wing extremism", a statistically significant difference can be observed only at levels of public opinion between zero and five percent. In substantial terms the difference is around one activity if the other variables are held at their median values.

Nevertheless, one should not forget that for all topics – independently of the election year effect – the opposition activities are significantly higher in statistical and substantial terms at high levels of public opinion than at low levels of public opinion.

The dummy controlling for the chancellorship of Helmut Kohl is only statistically significant for "unemployment". During the Kohl era the opposition was less active concerning the topic "unemployment" when controlling for the other variables. For all models in Table 9 the significant Wald χ^2 tests indicate that each model fits better than a constant only model. The fact that α is significantly different from zero indicates that overdispersion is present in the data and that therefore the negative binomial regression model is the right choice over a Poisson regression model. Testing for serial correlation in the residuals as described above reveals that introducing the lagged dependent variable solved the problem in all cases. Only the raw residuals of the "right-wing extremism" model show (negative) autocorrelation significant at the five percent level. The autoregressive Poisson model used as robustness check solves this problem. The results of these models are presented in the Appendix to this chapter. Comparing the results shows that the sign and the size of the coefficients as well as the statistical significance are quite robust for all five models. All variables keep their signs, and all variables that are statistically significant in Table 9 are also statistical with the autoregressive Poisson model. Two additional variables reach statistical significance in the "right-wing extremism" model, namely the interaction term and the "Kohl"-dummy.

Table 10 shows the results of the autoregressive negative binomial regressions, using the parliamentary activities of the government parties' parliamentary activities as dependent variable. The significant Wald χ^2 tests for all models again indicate that the independent variables add more information than a constant only model. The insignificant α for the "unemployment" and the "BSE" model suggests that a Poisson model without allowing for overdispersion would have been enough to fit the data. However, the results are not affected by the choice of using a negative binomial model.

The results reveal the following patterns: For the topics "right-wing extremism" and "BSE" a high level of parliamentary activities by the government parties in the immediate past only leads to the expectation of more parliamentary activities in the present. Oppositional activities in the previous month do not have a statistically significant impact on the overall number of government parties' parliamentary activities. Cabinet's parliamentary actions concerning "unemployment" and "right-wing extremism" significantly influence the activities of government's parliamentary party groups. One additional cabinet activity on the issue "unemployment" decreases the expected number of government parties' activities by 16 percent, holding all other variables constant. If the cabinet becomes active on the issue "right-wing extremism" one additional activity in the previous month is met by a 34 percent increase in government parties' parliamentary activities in the present, holding all other variables constant.

Table 10 Negative Binomial Regression of Government Parties' Parliamentary Activities

	Unemploy-ment	Foreigners	Pensions	Right-Wing Extremism	BSE
Gov. Parties' Parl. Activities $^{X}_{(t-1)}$	-0.160 (0.13)	0.062 (0.10)	0.149 (0.14)	0.711*** (0.24)	1.031** (0.47)
Oppositional Parl. Activities$_{(t-1)}$	-0.041 (0.04)	0.008 (0.01)	-0.031 (0.03)	-0.027 (0.04)	-0.056 (0.05)
Government's Parl. Activities$_{(t-1)}$	-0.172** (0.08)	0.048 (0.03)	0.036 (0.03)	0.291* (0.16)	-0.063 (0.26)
Public Opinion$_{(t-1)}$	0.868** (0.42)	1.568*** (0.41)	1.564 (1.83)	6.945*** (2.03)	4.768*** (1.27)
Election X PO$_{(t-1)}$	-0.333 (0.68)	2.212** (1.07)	-3.188 (4.18)	7.275 (4.88)	
Election Year	-0.165 (0.40)	-0.412* (0.23)	0.016 (0.31)	-0.503 (0.57)	-0.396 (0.50)
Kohl (6/1989-10/1998)	0.908*** (0.22)	1.427*** (0.21)	0.622*** (0.22)	0.743** (0.38)	0.692 (0.56)
Constant	-1.049*** (0.33)	-0.875*** (0.20)	-0.539* (0.29)	-1.803*** (0.45)	-2.016*** (0.62)
Wald $\chi^2(7)$	27.38***	175.79***	24.42***	62.90***	180.58***
α	0.1101	0.1457***	0.2282**	1.0824***	0.0000
N	196	196	196	196	196

^{X} The lagged dependent variable enters the equation in the following form: $\ln(y_{it-1} + 0.5)$; * significant at 10 percent ** at 5 percent *** at 1 percent; robust standard errors in parentheses; Wald $\chi^2(6)$ for the "BSE" model without the interaction term.

In years without a federal election the relationship between public opinion and activities is positive for all issues and only lacks statistical significance for the issue "pensions". The substantial effect lies between an increase of nine percent in the case of parliamentary activities concerning "unemployment" and an increase by factor two in the case of "right-wing extremism" when the number of people thinking that the issue belongs to the two most important problems increases by then percent, holding all other variables constant. The coefficient for the election year variable is negative for four of the five regression models but only statistically significant for the topic "foreigners". This indicates that in election years where the public does not see this issue as a problem government parties will spend fewer parliamentary activities on it.

The interaction term between public opinion and election year is only statistically significant for activities on the issue "foreigners". It has the expected positive sign: Government parties are more sensitive to public opinion during election years. Whether the difference between the reaction to public opinion in election and non-election years is statistically significant can again be best presented graphically. Figure 8 shows that for low levels of public opinion on the topic "foreigners" the parliamentary activities of government parties in the years before an upcoming election differ little from the respective activities during the rest of the legislative period. When the public opinion variables take values between zero and two percent, government parties do significantly less. However, this means only 0.7 fewer activities on average. Once the public opinion variable takes values of 37 percent and above, government parties will become significantly more active in election years than in non-election years. When 75 percent of the population deem the issue "foreigners" one of the two most important problems facing the country, government parties will on average engage in 16 more parliamentary activities in election years, namely overall 23 instead of seven. For the topic "right-wing extremism" the effect is similar, but there is no significant difference between the reactions with or without an election close by.

One can see that government parties react in the same way to public opinion on the topics "foreigners" and "right-wing extremism" as do opposition parties. This is not true for the topics "unemployment" and "pensions", however. While a higher proportion of concerned voters still leads to more parliamentary activities, as one would expect from Hypothesis 1, the relationship between election years and non-election years is not in line with Hypothesis 3: Concerning "unemployment" and "pensions", the government's parliamentary party groups are less active in election years than in non-election years. As one can see in Figure 8 the difference is statistically significant, as the 90 percent confidence interval does not include the zero for the issue "unemployment", when between 47 and 80 percent of the respondents report that "unemployment" is either the most or the second most important problem. This is the case around 50 percent of the time during the period studied here. However, the difference is rather insignificant in substantial terms as the difference is on average at most "half an activity" when holding the other variables at their median values. For "pensions" the difference is statistically insignificant over the whole observed range.

Figure 8 Difference in Expected Number of Government Parties' Activities in Election and non-Election Years

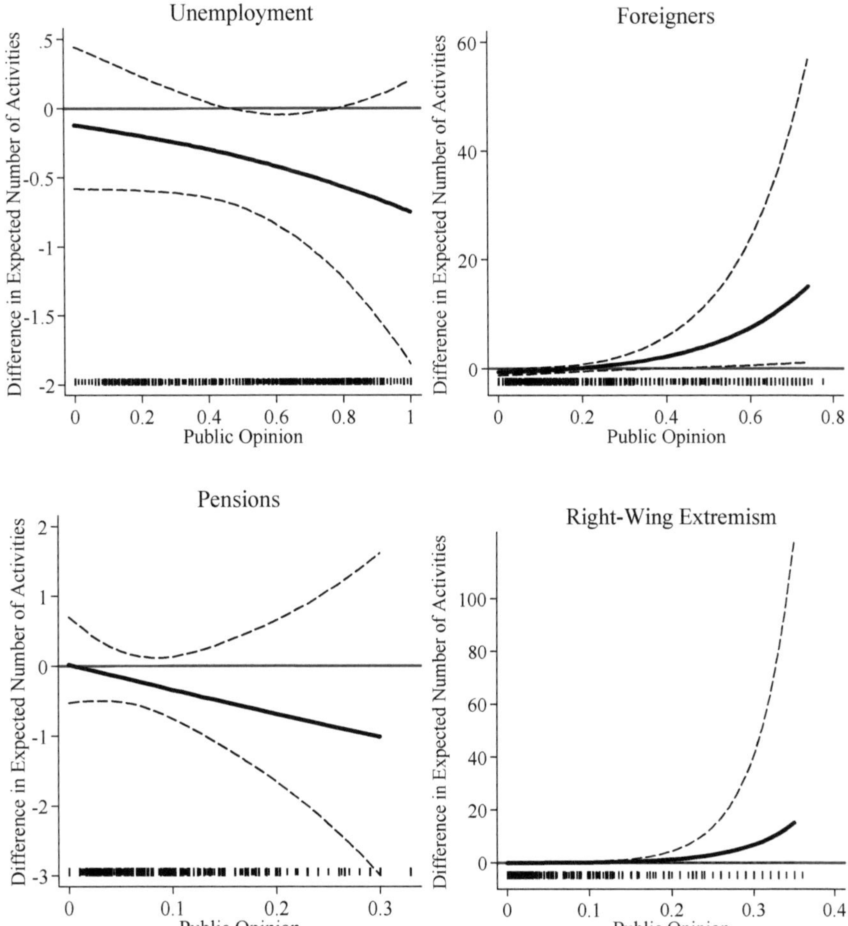

Note: Dashed line shows the 90 percent confidence interval; all other variables were set to their median values. The histogram at the bottom of each graph shows the distribution of the public opinion variable.

The "Kohl"-dummy is positive and statistically significant for all issues with the exception of "BSE". The parliamentary party groups CDU/CSU and FDP were more active on these issues than their successors of the SPD and the Greens. This change in activity levels could be evidence for a shift in issue attention, which in turn would be a result of the change of government due to shifts in issue salience. Alternatively, the repartition of work between government and parliamentary majority might have changed. The results of the autoregressive Poisson model allowing for overdispersion which I described above confirm the results discussed so far with the exception that government parties' activities on "right-wing extremism" do no longer depend significantly on the previous values of cabinet activities. In addition, the public opinion variable in the "BSE" model loses its statistical significance. However, one should consider here that there was no evidence of serial correlation in the raw residuals and in the Pearson residuals in the static model. Therefore no adjustment to autocorrelation is actually needed.[90]

All count dependent variables for cabinet's parliamentary activities on the different issues show clear signs of overdispersion as indicated by the values of α presented in Table 11, which are significantly different from zero in all models. Compared to the models that explain the parliamentary activities of opposition and government parties, the models for cabinet's parliamentary activities are worse in fitting the data. The insignificant Wald χ^2 tests indicate that we cannot exclude that the coefficients of all variables, except the intercept, are simultaneously zero in the models on cabinet activities regarding "unemployment",[91] "foreigners", and "pensions". In each of the models for "foreigners" and "pensions" only one variable reaches the ten percent level of statistical significance, while all other variables are statistically insignificant. Hence, there is at best weak evidence that cabinet reacts in the expected way to public opinion (at least in non-election years) on the issue "foreigners" and that the Kohl cabinet showed more activities on the issue "pensions" than its successor cabinet under Chancellor Schröder. For "unemployment" the coefficients for these two variables, public opinion and the Kohl dummy, are positive and statistically significant. The "BSE" model results suggest that cabinet's parliamentary activities were more pronounced during election years and during the Schröder era. It is likely that these variables rather take up time effects of the BSE crisis rather than substantial differences in dealing with the issue by different governments.

---

90 In the static negative binomial regression model the results for public opinion in the "BSE" model are robust. The coefficient is even larger (6.567) and statistically significant at the one percent level.

91 When excluding the lagged dependent variable, which is not necessary to control for autocorrelation, the Wald χ^2 test is significant at the ten percent level.

Table 11 Negative Binomial Regression of Government's Parliamentary Activities

	Unemployment	Foreigners	Pensions	Right-Wing Extremism	BSE
Government's Parl. Activities $^{X}_{(t-1)}$	-0.097 (0.15)	-0.018 (0.10)	0.012 (0.08)	-13.547*** (0.64)	0.256 (0.26)
Oppositional Parl. Activities$_{(t-1)}$	-0.064 (0.05)	0.002 (0.02)	0.026 (0.03)	0.039 (0.07)	0.022 (0.07)
Gov. Parties' Parl. Activities$_{(t-1)}$	-0.049 (0.10)	-0.053 (0.06)	-0.006 (0.07)	0.167 (0.29)	0.121 (0.42)
Public Opinion$_{(t-1)}$	1.678*** (0.56)	1.192* (0.63)	-1.562 (1.65)	6.341** (3.00)	1.873 (1.42)
Election X PO$_{(t-1)}$	-1.129 (0.91)	0.437 (1.61)	3.015 (3.33)	-10.189* (5.67)	
Election Year	0.433 (0.58)	0.353 (0.29)	0.024 (0.27)	1.792*** (0.50)	0.642* (0.34)
Kohl (6/1989-10/1998)	0.405* (0.24)	-0.149 (0.22)	0.359* (0.20)	0.036 (0.74)	-0.683** (0.33)
Constant	-1.145*** (0.42)	0.079 (0.19)	0.580** (0.26)	-12.483*** (0.67)	-0.921*** (0.23)
α	0.9863***	0.7189***	0.7110***	3.3925***	1.1990***
Wald $\chi^2(7)$	11.29	6.57	8.13	1073.55***	46.19***
N	196	196	196	196	196

X The lagged dependent variable enters the equation in the following form $\ln(y_{it-1} + 0.5)$; * significant at 10 percent ** at 5 percent *** at 1 percent; robust standard errors in parentheses; Wald $\chi^2(6)$ for the "BSE" model without the interaction term.

Only activities on "right-wing extremism" depend on past activities: If the cabinet showed some activity in the previous month on the issue, it is unlikely to take up the topic again the following month. When federal elections are more than twelve months away, the effect of public opinion on cabinet activities concerning "right-wing extremism" is in line with the expectations. More concern leads to more activities. During election years, however, cabinet will rather react with fewer parliamentary activities to more pronounced public attention to the problem. Yet, the difference between the reaction in election years and non-election years is only statistically significant for low levels of public problem awareness (between zero and seven percent), as can be seen in Figure 9.

Holding all other variables at their median, this statistically significant effect only results in an additional 0.25 activities on average in election years if the topic "right-wing extremism" does not fare among the most important problems for anyone. For higher levels of public attention government is, on average, less active in election years than in non-election years. The difference is not statistically significant, however. For the issue "unemployment" the results as displayed in Figure 9 also go against the direction expected in Hypothesis 3, but just as for "foreigners" and "pensions" the difference between election years and non-election years is insignificant over the entire range of public opinion.

Some results fail the robustness check of the autoregressive Poisson model.[92] However, one should again keep in mind that serial correlation is not a problem that has to be dealt with in these models. The theoretical considerations that led to Hypothesis 2 (government reacts the least and the slowest of all political actors) could imply that a different lag structure should be chosen for the government model. Including a time lag of two months for the public opinion variable and the activities of the other actors indeed improves the overall model fit of the regressions. Only the model with government activities on "pensions" just barely fails statistical significance at the ten percent level. The public opinion variable now has the expected positive sign in all models, but still fails statistical significance in the "pensions" model. The other results stay mostly robust. In addition to the factors discussed above, also the past activities of opposition and parliamentary majority have a significant impact on government activities. More/fewer opposition activities on "unemployment" or "pensions" two months ago are associated with fewer/more government activities in the present. The same relationship can be found for activities of the parliamentary majority and cabinet activities on the issue "foreigners".

---

92 The public opinion variable loses its statistical significance for the issues "foreigners" and "right-wing extremism"; the same is true for the interaction term in the "right-wing extremism" model.

Figure 9 Difference in Expected Number of Government Activities in Election and non-Election Years

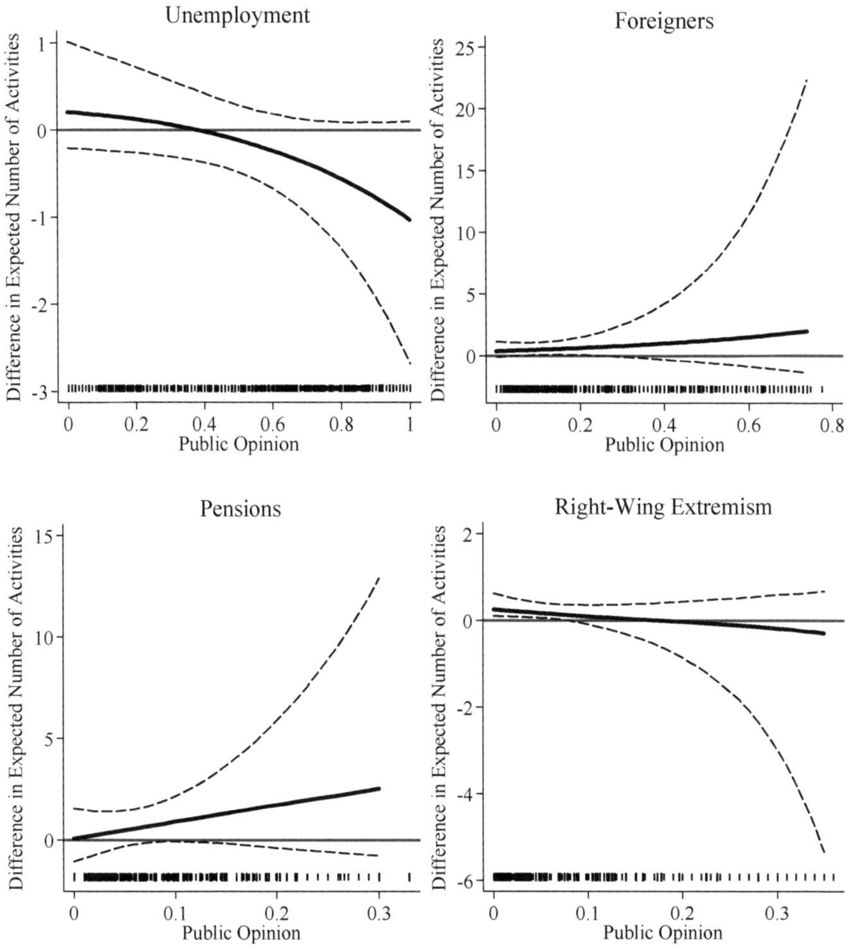

Note: Dashed line shows the 90 percent confidence interval; all other variables were set to their median values. The histogram at the bottom of each graph shows the distribution of the public opinion variable.

3.3.5 Discussion

Overall, there is considerable evidence for Hypothesis 1: Public opinion indeed seems to influence the parliamentary activities of political actors in a systematic way. When the public cares intensely about an issue, parliamentary actors are more likely to take up the issue in their parliamentary activities. This relationship is found in non-election years for all issues considered here in the case of oppositional activities and for four out of five issues for activities of the parliamentary majority. For the government this relationship is still visible for three out of these five issues. The differences between the political actors' responsiveness is in line with the expectations formulated in Hypothesis 2. Opposition, for which responsive behavior was assumed to be the easiest, indeed responds to public opinion on all issues analyzed in this chapter.

The parliamentary majority also shows responsive behavior on all issues but "pensions". A number of plausible explanations suggest themselves for the exception of "pensions". One explanation might be that responses to this specific problem are quite technical and therefore rather left to the government to respond to. Another explanation might be that MPs of one of the government parties avoid asking difficult questions to their government in times when general public attention is highest, and rather respond to their local constituencies. When pressured by their constituency government MPs might even have incentives to strategically delay asking such questions until the public attention has shifted to another issue. However, it is not clear why such a strategy should foremost be used concerning the topic "pensions". Concerning "unemployment" voters are as likely to hold the government responsible for problems. The overall lower levels of public attention to the "pensions" problem might make an evasive strategy easier. Last but not least, the timing of bill sponsorship might be determined rather by government's strategic considerations than by an independent decision of the government majorities. This can be seen by the fact that a considerable number of bills concerning the topic of "pensions" were handed out by government. Depending on the legislative period, between 38 and 64 percent of all bills on the topic are identical with government initiatives and introduced parallel in the Bundestag and the Bundesrat in order to save time in the legislative process.

According to the regression results government is the least responsive of the three political actors that were distinguished in this chapter. However, government activities still respond to the level of public problem awareness in three of the five issues. Only for "pensions" and "BSE" the positive significant relationship expected from Hypothesis 1 cannot be confirmed. For pensions even a negative sign can be found for the coefficient of the public opinion variable. Yet, this does not necessarily mean that government does not care about what the public thinks. Table 14 in the Appendix indicates that there might be another reason for the "non-finding" of responsiveness of government to public concern on pensions: In no other issue discussed in this chapter government shows more activities. Most of these bills and regulations are just small technical adjustments, which do not attract public attention. These routine activities dominate any other potentially short-term responsive activities.

Similarly, one cannot blame government inactivity in the case of "BSE". The lack of responsiveness becomes less problematic from a normative perspective, if one considers that the government (as well as parliamentary majority and opposition) had the problem BSE on the parliamentary agenda even before the public perceived BSE as one of the major problems. While opposition activities and also activities of the parliamentary majority explode once the problem is in the focus of the public and rapidly fade away thereafter, government activities reach a local maximum one month after the peak of public attention, but the issue stays on the government agenda quite constantly afterwards. A positive interpretation would not see a problem of non-responsiveness but claim that government does not suddenly shift its attention to public concerns in a populist manner. In addition, the timing of some of the government activities are externally given, such as EU directives that have to be transposed or communications of government that are sometimes asked for by parliament. Overall, one can state that opposition responds the fastest and most flexible to shifts in public opinion, which is in line with Hypothesis 2. As discussed above this does not, however, necessarily imply that government and parliamentary majority fail to consider public opinion in policy-making.

The results discussed so far concerned non-election years. In election years the picture is more complex. Hypothesis 3 stated that higher levels of responsiveness to public opinion can be expected shortly before elections. Clear evidence for this relationship could be found for the opposition. For all topics fewer oppositional activities were found in election years when the public opinion surveys showed low problem awareness of the voters. This could indicate that opposition shifts resources to more urgent and electorally salient topics in election years. Significant differences at high levels of public opinion could only be found for the issue "unemployment", where opposition activities are significantly higher in election years than in non-election years. This shows that opposition parties indeed employ their parliamentary activities strategically. At high levels of public problem awareness, however, they usually react no matter whether elections are close or not.

For governments and their parliamentary majorities there is little evidence for such strategic employment of parliamentary activities. The same pattern is only visible for the issue "foreigners" for the parliamentary majority. For the issue "unemployment" the relationship is reverse and for the other issues there is no significant difference at all. For government none of the issues shows the hypothesized relationship. Instead, low levels of attention lead to significantly more activities on the issue "right-wing extremism" in election years in comparison to non-election years. The reasons that there is almost no evidence of strategic usage of parliamentary activities as hypothesized are probably the same that were already discussed above. Routine activities and the need to provide policy change instead of just putting issues on the agenda limit the possibilities of responsiveness. Before elections government parties might refrain even more from asking critical questions on issues such as "unemployment" or "pensions", where government could be made responsible for the lack of solutions to the problem.

The control variables do not reveal clear patterns. There is little systematic evidence for the influence of one actor's activities on the activities of others. Most evidence can be found for a dampening effect on parliamentary activities by parliamentary majority and opposition when government has dealt with an issue in the previous period. Likewise, there is an increase in their activities when government neglects an issue. This is in line with the view of government as a problem solver and of parliament, especially opposition, as an instance of control that puts issues on the agenda when government does not deal with an important issue. The lack of evidence for dynamics between parliamentary actors stands against the findings of Vliegenthart et al. (2011), who find such dynamics in agenda-setting of Belgian parties. One important reason for the different results is probably the level of aggregation of the data: Vliegenthart et al. (2011) use weekly data at the level of individual parties, which is better suited to find such effects.

The different levels of activities revealed by the dummy for government composition might point at differences in the saliency of issues for different governments. Holding all other factors constant, the conservative Kohl government showed more activities concerning "unemployment" and "pensions", while the left opposition showed less interest in the issue "unemployment". However, as demonstrated by the example of "BSE", this dummy could also capture some time effects or a different division of labor between government and its parliamentary majority.

3.4 Conclusion

This chapter has dealt with questions concerning the responsiveness of political actors and their parliamentary activities to public opinion, and especially with the differences between government, its parliamentary majority, and opposition. Normative as well as vote-seeking considerations lead to the expectation that political actors should respond to the policy priorities of the public, as reflected, for instance, in the "most important problem" question. Simply plotting the number of parliamentary activities on the topics "unemployment", "foreigners", "pensions", "right-wing extremism", and "BSE" and the percentage of respondents who deem the respective topic a "most important problem" shows that the two variables are clearly correlated. With the help of vector autoregressive models it could be established that the central causal direction is, as expected, from public opinion to parliamentary activities.

Results of negative-binomial time series regression with the number of parliamentary activities on a topic per month as dependent variable showed that there is indeed a close relationship between public opinion and parliamentary activities. However, there are differences between the various political actors: Higher levels of public attention are indeed related to higher activity levels of the opposition. With restrictions this is also true for the government parties in parliament. As expected this direct connection is less clear for government. Differences in responsiveness to public opinion depending on the closeness of elections can be shown especially for the opposition. The result that opposition parties take public opinion more into account in election years shows that parliamentary activities are not only used to fulfill normative expectations, but they are also employed instrumentally in order to win votes. Hence, what we observe is not simply congruence between elected and representatives due to the influence of some unobserved variable but rather suggests strategic responsiveness.

This chapter provides good evidence that bills and other parliamentary activities are a means to react in a responsive manner to public opinion in Germany. Signaling to the voters that their concerns and priorities are shared can help win voters on the next elections. In Germany, parties dominate most parliamentary activities. In other systems individual MPs have more leeway to use parliamentary activities such as bill introduction for personal vote-seeking. Such a perspective will be adopted in Chapter 4.

3.5 Appendix to Chapter 3

I. Number of Parliamentary Activities on the Selected Issues by the Different Initiators

Table 12 Parliamentary Activities Concerning "Unemployment" by Initiator (LP 11-15)[93]

	Govern-ment	Gov. Parties	Oppo-sition	Mixed	Total
Bills	28	26	25	1	80
Ordinances	2	-	-	-	2
Gov. Declarations	31	-	-	-	31
Communication of Gov.	115	-	-	-	115
Motions	-	16	110	4	130
Motions for a Resolution	-	5	54	0	59
Major Interpellations	-	3	22	1	26
Minor Interpellations	-	2	142	0	144
Oral Questions	-	23	187	0	210
Urgent Questions	-	0	1	0	1
Written Questions	-	102	475	0	577
Total	176	177	1016	6	1375

[93] In the following tables the parliamentary activities of the entire legislative periods 11 to 15 between 1987 and 2005 are presented. The analysis, however, is restricted to the period 1989 to 2005 due to missing public opinion data.

Table 13 Parliamentary Activities Concerning "Foreigners/Asylum Seekers" by Initiator (LP 11-15)

	Government	Gov. Parties	Opposition	Mixed	Total
Bills	74	27	63	3	167
Ordinances	34	-	-	-	34
Gen. Admin. Regulations	10	-	-	-	10
Gov. Declarations	32	-	-	-	32
Communication of Gov.	129	-	-	-	129
Motions	-	19	195	17	231
Motions for a Resolution	-	12	75	3	90
Major Interpellations	-	9	31	1	41
Minor Interpellations	-	0	702	2	704
Oral Questions	-	93	241	0	334
Urgent Questions	-	0	9	0	9
Written Questions	-	340	726	0	1066
Total	279	500	2042	26	2847

Table 14 Parliamentary Activities Concerning "Pensions" by Initiator (LP 11-15)

	Government	Gov. Parties	Opposition	Mixed	Total
Bills	113	53	27	10	203
Ordinances	164	-	-	-	164
Gen. Admin. Regulations	5	-	-	-	5
Gov. Declarations	18	-	-	-	18
Communication of Gov.	230	-	-	-	230

Motions	-	9	102	7	118
Motions for a Resolution	-	7	72	1	80
Major Interpellations	-	0	13	0	13
Minor Interpellations	-	0	114	0	114
Oral Questions	-	25	102	0	127
Urgent Questions	-	0	3	0	3
Written Questions	-	124	485	0	609
Total	530	218	918	18	1684

Table 15 Parliamentary Activities Concerning "Right-Wing Extremism" by Initiator (LP 11-15)

	Govern-ment	Gov. Parties	Oppo-sition	Mixed	Total
Bills	1	0	4	0	5
Gov. Declarations	4	-	-	-	4
Communication of Gov.	22	-	-	-	22
Motion	-	6	24	6	36
Motions for a Resolution	-	2	13	0	15
Major Interpellations	-	2	6	1	9
Minor Interpellations	-	0	509	0	509
Oral Questions	-	13	102	0	115
Urgent Questions	-	0	1	0	1
Written Questions	-	51	271	0	322
Total	27	74	930	7	1038

Table 16 Parliamentary Activities Concerning "BSE" by Initiator (LP 11-15)

	Govern-ment	Gov. Parties	Oppo-sition	Mixed	Total
Bills	2	1	0	0	3
Ordinances	37	-	-	-	37
Gov. Declarations	2	-	-	-	2
Communication of Gov.	32	-	-	-	32
Motions	-	6	19	2	27
Motions for a Resolution	-	2	7	0	9
Major Interpellations	-	0	4	0	4
Minor Interpellations	-	0	19	0	19
Oral Questions	-	8	21	0	29
Written Questions	-	11	83	0	94
Total	41	28	153	2	256

II. Autoregressive Poisson Models as Robustness Checks

Table 17 Autoregressive Poisson Results for Opposition Party Activities

	Unemploy-ment	Foreigners	Right-Wing Extremism	Pension	BSE
Gov. Parties' Parl. Activities$_{(t-1)}$	-0.065 (0.06)	0.005 (0.02)	-0.048 (0.05)	-0.002 (0.05)	0.251 (0.16)
Government's Parl. Activities$_{(t-1)}$	-0.114** (0.05)	-0.047* (0.03)	0.123 (0.10)	-0.026 (0.02)	-0.071 (0.21)
Public Opinion$_{(t-1)}$	0.552** (0.27)	0.879*** (0.28)	4.051*** (0.83)	2.473** (0.99)	4.352*** (0.81)
Election X PO$_{(t-1)}$	1.185** (0.48)	1.239 (0.92)	3.832* (1.95)	0.986 (2.43)	
Election Year	-0.608* (0.33)	-0.377** (0.15)	-0.418** (0.17)	-0.281 (0.20)	-0.219 (0.32)
Kohl (6/1989-10/1998)	-0.412*** (0.10)	0.104 (0.10)	0.247** (0.11)	-0.196 (0.12)	-0.117 (0.28)
ρ_1	0.299*** (0.07)	0.172** (0.07)	0.273*** (0.07)	0.023 (0.08)	0.240*** (0.06)
Constant	1.455*** (0.18)	2.120*** (0.08)	1.233*** (0.11)	1.457*** (0.14)	-0.465** (0.23)
N	196	196	196	196	196

Table 18 Autoregressive Poisson Results for Parliamentary Majority Activities

	Unemployment	Foreigners	Right-Wing Extremism	Pension	BSE
Oppositional Parl. Activities$_{(t-1)}$	-0.038 (0.03)	0.005 (0.01)	0.001 (0.04)	-0.032 (0.03)	0.101 (0.06)
Government's Parl. Activities$_{(t-1)}$	-0.167* (0.09)	0.052 (0.04)	0.086 (0.26)	0.031 (0.03)	-0.025 (0.31)
Public Opinion$_{(t-1)}$	0.821* (0.42)	1.631*** (0.35)	5.601** (2.33)	1.551 (1.85)	1.756 (1.69)
Election X PO$_{(t-1)}$	-0.319 (0.77)	2.444* (1.26)	12.206** (5.10)	-2.981 (4.27)	
Election Year	-0.152 (0.48)	-0.457* (0.27)	-0.736 (0.59)	-0.036 (0.29)	-0.400 (0.53)
Kohl (6/1989-10/1998)	0.852*** (0.21)	1.500*** (0.21)	0.777* (0.41)	0.681*** (0.21)	0.862 (0.53)
ρ_1	-0.128* (0.07)	0.020 (0.08)	0.223*** (0.07)	0.119 (0.07)	0.248*** (0.06)
Constant	-1.000*** (0.33)	-0.870*** (0.21)	-2.009*** (0.44)	-0.525* (0.28)	-2.745*** (0.49)
N	196	196	196	196	196

Table 19 Autoregressive Poisson Results for Government Activities

	Unemployment	Foreigners	Right-Wing Extremism	Pension	BSE
Oppositional Parl. Activities$_{(t-1)}$	-0.061 (0.04)	0.004 (0.02)	0.009 (0.09)	0.030 (0.03)	0.021 (0.08)
Gov. Parties' Parl. Activities$_{(t-1)}$	-0.019 (0.12)	-0.044 (0.06)	0.066 (0.32)	-0.018 (0.07)	0.009 (0.42)
Public Opinion$_{(t-1)}$	1.543*** (0.55)	1.010 (0.76)	6.112 (4.86)	-1.382 (2.01)	2.839 (1.88)
Election X PO$_{(t-1)}$	-1.077 (0.98)	0.358 (1.96)	-6.729 (9.59)	2.480 (3.54)	
Election Year	0.413 (0.63)	0.351 (0.31)	1.518** (0.74)	0.084 (0.27)	0.632* (0.34)
Kohl (6/1989-10/1998)	0.320 (0.24)	-0.123 (0.22)	-0.170 (0.60)	0.388* (0.20)	-0.651* (0.35)
ρ_1	-0.053 (0.07)	-0.051 (0.08)	-0.074 (0.07)	0.015 (0.07)	0.058 (0.07)
Constant	-1.043** (0.42)	0.058 (0.21)	-2.849*** (0.73)	0.542** (0.27)	-0.998*** (0.27)
N	196	196	196	196	196

4 Private Members' Bills between Party and Constituency

So far bill introduction has been treated as a collective activity in this study. The formal model of bill introduction presented in Chapter 2 shows that opposition parties have an incentive to introduce bills in order to signal their position to voters. This is true as long as voters make their voting decision based on the perceived policy positions of parties and if they see bills as credible signals of these positions. In the formal model as well as in the subsequent empirical applications up to this point, I have treated parties as unitary actors. This approach has a long tradition in research on parliamentary democracies. Considering the high level of party cohesion especially in systems where the survival of government depends on the support of its parliamentary majority, this simplifying assumption of parties as unitary actors can be justified in a wide range of applications. Especially when considering the success of bills political parties are the natural level of analysis in parliamentary democracies.

Yet bill introduction is an individual right in most parliamentary democracies[94] and also in parliamentary systems individual MPs have incentives to deviate from the party line in order to pursue a policy agenda on their own. Electoral incentives in particular can encourage MPs to build up a personal reputation independent of the party label. The costs of deviating from the party line can be very high, however: Voting down a government bill could put the survival of government at risk. Therefore roll-call vote analysis mostly reveals the government-opposition divide in parliamentary systems. However, parliamentarians have a wider range of options to develop a personal profile and to distinguish themselves from the party in order to strengthen their chances of reelection.

---

94 The German case is a well known exception. In the German Bundestag bill introduction is a collective right. The right of initiating legislation from within parliament lies in the hands of parliamentary party groups or groups of MPs comprising at least five percent of the parliamentarians. Therefore the possibilities to use bills as signals of individual positions are limited. In all other countries discussed in more detail in this dissertation (Belgium, France, and United Kingdom), parliamentarians have the individual right of bill introduction. Germany is also exceptional in this respect when taking a broader comparative perspective: While also some other West-European countries, namely Austria, Italy, and Spain, demand more than one MP to introduce a bill, the numerical restrictions are the most severe in Germany (compare Mattson 1995: 458).

Speeches, parliamentary questions, or bill sponsorship are less costly signals as they do not endanger government survival directly and should therefore provide better opportunities to signal dissent. In this chapter, I will focus on private members' bills as a means for MPs to signal a position deviating from the party line or to signal different policy priorities to the voters in their constituency. Individual incentives for bill introduction in parliamentary democracies have not yet received much attention in research. There is neither a stringent theoretical model of private members' bill introduction, nor an empirical analysis of systematic patterns of bill sponsorship in parliamentary democracies. This research will deal with both aspects to close this gap.

Even though prior research on bill introduction is rare, I can build on research on other forms of individual legislative behavior, especially voting behavior, where the incentive structure can be expected to be at least partly related. The individual incentives for an MP to use private members' bills as a policy signal to his constituency are expected to depend on a number of factors, most prominently electoral incentives, party organization, and individual attributes. In this chapter, I present a formal model of private members' bill introduction as an act of deviation from the party line. Empirical testable hypotheses are derived from this model. The central empirical test case will be the bill sponsorship behavior of French MPs of the Assemblée Nationale between 1997 and 2002. The election in single member districts together with the comparatively unrestricted possibilities of bill introduction make France a promising case to find the predicted patterns.

In the following, I will first review the literature on the incentives to deviate from party line and on the usage of bill introduction for that purpose. Then I will present a formal model of bill introduction as deviation from party line, derive empirical implications from the model and test these empirically on the case of France. The final section concludes.

4.1 Incentives for Individual Legislative Behavior

As I have already argued, research on legislation in parliamentary democracies most often focuses on the legislative output and concentrates on government and the parliamentary majority, while neglecting the opposition. The chapters so far have deviated from this "mainstream" research agenda by focusing on the motivations of parliamentary opposition to introduce bills as signals of their policy position and as reaction to public opinion. In this chapter, I take another turn off the main road of research on legislation in parliamentary democracies: Instead of considering parties as unitary actors as the unit of analysis, I will elaborate on the individual incentives of MPs to introduce legislation. I understand bill introduction by individual MPs as a vote-seeking tool by arguing that MPs can use bills as a public signal of deviation from the official party line.

Traditionally research on parliamentary systems has focused on political parties whereas research on congress was more concerned with individual legislators (Mezey 1994). Consequently one can primarily build on literature on the US Congress for theoretical and empirical evidence for individual legislative behavior. In order to understand why elected representatives take a certain action, in our case introduce bills, we have to look at their incentives. If we take reelection as one of the major goals of politicians (Mayhew 1974: 6), introducing bills should be associated with positive payoffs if it increases the politicians' chances to reach this goal. Benefits from introducing bills are hence related to the concept of a personal vote as defined by Cain, Ferejohn, and Fiorina (1987: 9): "The personal vote refers to that portion of a candidate's electoral support which originates in his or her personal qualities, qualifications, activities, and record."

The connection between legislative behavior and voters can be twofold. On the one hand legislative voting has been found to be influenced by constituency preferences (e.g. Froman 1963, Flinn 1964); on the other hand the legislative voting record influences voters' decisions (e.g. Miller and Stokes 1963, Fiorina 1974, Erikson 1978, Bartels 1991, Ansolabehere et al. 2001). These studies all use roll-call data and have made the connection between election results and legislative behavior in the US context. For my purpose of studying bill sponsorship behavior, it is of special interest to identify the factors influencing the legislative behavior of representatives and to consider their transferability. For individual representatives constituency (e.g. Froman 1963, Flinn 1964) and party pressure (e.g. Mayhew 1966), but also idiosyncratic factors such as career development (e.g. Stratmann 2000), gender (e.g. Welch 1985, Clark 1998)[95], or minority status (e.g. Whitby 2002) have been identified to influence the voting decision. Most studies find a number of factors influencing voting behavior. Especially the expectations of party and constituency influence the voting behavior of representatives. Stratmann (2000) finds evidence that early on in their careers legislators are not familiar with their constituency's position on all issues, hence freshmen in Congress are more likely to trust party cues than more senior legislators. He also finds evidence that after redistricting legislators adapt their legislative behavior according to the preferences of their new constituency. Crespin (2010) adds an interesting twist to that result: While voting behavior changes on

95 Schwindt-Bayer and Rosetta (2004), however, find that the gender effect of roll-call voting disappears once one controls for party and constituency influences.

visible votes after redistricting, it does not change on procedural votes that are mostly only recognized by an internal audience. The research question of why individual representatives show a certain voting behavior has especially been dealt with in the US context; in non-Congress research on voting behavior questions of party cohesion and cleavages on the system level predominate (compare Collie 1984 for an overview, Rosenthal and Voeten 2004 on the French Fourth Republic, and also newer comparative research e.g. Sieberer 2006 and Carey 2007). As an exception of the rule some recent research has changed the perspective: Kam (2009) takes both perspectives – party and individual – into account, and Sieberer (2010) analyzes the effect of the mixed member electoral system in Germany on deviation from the party line. He finds evidence that district MPs are more likely to deviate from the party line but cannot relate this to deviating district preferences.

There is also some evidence for a personal vote in European parliamentary systems. Lindon and Weill (1974) find indications for a personal vote as well as a party vote in France. However, a number of authors doubt that parliamentary work has any significant impact on the personal vote. Norton and Wood (1993), for instance, claim that instead of parliamentary behavior the MP's constituency service efforts are responsible for the personal vote. Building my argument, I follow Kam (2009), who challenges this view. In his study of party dissent in the Westminster democracies Great Britain, Canada, Australia, and New Zealand, Kam argues that dissenting voting behavior in parliament had about the same personal vote effect as constituency service. In addition to electoral pressures, career ambitions and also sociological factors play a central role in explaining dissent according to Kam.

In addition to roll-call votes also other forms of legislative behavior have been analyzed. The advantage of analyzing other forms of legislative behavior for the purpose of transferring results to the problem of explaining individual bill sponsorship behavior might be a higher comparability. Deviation from the party line can be very costly especially in parliamentary democracies where losing a vote on a government proposal could mean the end of government and the dissolution of parliament. Therefore voting is under strict party control to enforce party discipline. Concerning other less costly forms of legislative behavior individual legislators enjoy more freedom. Analyzing other forms of legislative behavior potentially has additional advantages over roll-call vote analysis: In parliamentary democracies in particular roll-call data often is not available at all or roll-call votes are only held after being requested, which might follow strategic considerations and imply selection bias (Hug 2010). Even when these problems are overcome, the high level of party discipline in voting might hide underlying differences within parties. Studies focusing on other forms of legislative behavior are presented below.

Becher and Sieberer (2008) examine defection from the party line using data on the "explanation of vote" that MPs in the German Bundestag can use to justify their voting behavior. These oral or written statements have the advantage of being more nuanced than actual voting behavior. An MP could vote with his party and still signal discontent with the decision taken. According to Becher and Sieberer holding an executive or parliamentary office reduces the likelihood of defection. The mode of election does not have the expected effect – district partisans are less instead of more likely to deviate – but high competition in a district increases the probability of an "explanation of vote" deviating from the party line.

Maltzman and Sigelman (1996) argue that the usage of one- and five-minute speeches in Congress is not well explained by electoral explanations. Instead they suggest that these speeches serve as potential policy influence tools within Congress. Victor (2011) examines legislative speech to find evidence for the effect of higher office-seeking on policy specialization. Her research indicates that politicians are motivated by elections: During their careers ambitious legislators specialize on specific issues to signal competence and expertise. When campaigning for higher office, however, they signal less specialization in order to win a broader constituency. Bernauer and Bräuninger (2009) use parliamentary speeches to identify differences in positions of individual legislators in the German Bundestag. They show that intra-party group membership relates to how legislators deviate from the positions of their party leaders. Proksch and Slapin (2010) model the allocation of speech time to MPs as a strategic decision of party leaders who on the one hand value party unity and on the other hand want the MPs of their party group to be publically visible in order to increase their chances of reelection. MPs have to decide strategically whether to represent the official party line in their speech or whether to signal a deviating position due to personal preferences or to deviating views in their constituency. From their model, Proksch and Slapin derive the expectation that directly elected MPs in Germany, who have a higher incentive to use legislative speech to signal a deviating position to their constituency, are less likely to be given speaking time on the floor. They find empirical evidence in support of this expectation. Their model and the empirical evidence for it suggest that depending on the institutional setting, one cannot directly infer positions or party unity from the observed positions of speeches. This has the important implication that alternative measures of legislative behavior might have similar problems as roll-call vote analysis.

Early day motions in the British parliament are another potential source to measure the position and priorities of MPs (Franklin and Tappin 1977, Leece and Berrington 1977). Early day motions can be used to signal an opinion by MPs without restrictions on the issue or time of submission.[96] Just as research on other forms of legislative behavior has shown, also the analysis of early day motions reveals individual patterns of legislative activities.[97] When given the chance, MPs use the possibility to distinguish themselves from their colleagues/party in order to gain attention or to reach particularistic goals.

Parliamentary questions could be another tool to gain publicity or to show concern for the interest of constituents (compare Wiberg 1995: 181).

Stratmann and Baur (2002) find evidence for the effect of the electoral rule on legislative behavior in Germany: MPs, who were elected on the party list, choose committees where they can serve the (non-geographic) party constituency, while the MPs, who were elected directly in an electoral district can be found in committees in which they can provide "pork" to their geographic constituency.

Literature on the incentives of individual MPs to introduce bills is rare. To my knowledge there is no systematic study on the context of European parliamentary democracies. Some authors, however, treat bill sponsorship (e.g. Schiller 1995, Whitby 2002, Barnello and Bratton 2007, Woon 2008, Rocca and Sanchez 2008, Rocca and Gordon 2010, Wilson 2010) or bill co-sponsorship (e.g. Campbell 1982, Kessler and Krehbiel 1996, Harward and Moffett 2010) in the US Congress. Many of these articles are concerned with the content of bills, or the influence of gender or minority background on the propensity to sponsor minority-specific bills. These studies have interesting implications for descrip-

---

96 Early day motions deal with all kinds of subjects from wishing luck for the "England Football Team" (EDM 2341, session 05-06) over "Support for English Strawberries" (EDM 2334, session 05-06) to more serious issues like "Climate Change" (EDM 178, session 05-06) or "Parliamentary approval for participation in armed conflict" (EDM 85, session 05-06). All early day motions since the session 1989/1990 can be found online on http://edmi.parliament.uk/EDMi/, accessed on 10 February 2011. Formally, the MP must submit a title and a sentence of no more than 250 words, which can be signed by other MPs in order to show their support. Some motions are signed by hundreds of colleagues; the majority of early day motions, however, are only signed by one or two MPs. Most of the early day motions are never debated in parliament, but they frequently receive public attention and media coverage (House of Commons 2010a).

97 Even though the recent data on early day motions is quite easily accessible and the data promises to provide information on MPs positions relatively independent of partisan influence, there are only few articles actually using this data. Nason (2001) produced some unpublished work in which he finds evidence for party, regional, gender, and age structure in signing the early day motions. Childs and Withey (2004) find evidence for women's inclination to co-sign early day motions on women and feminist issues.

tive and substantive representation and for the question why certain issues are chosen, but they do not (intend to) answer the puzzle of why representatives sponsor bills that will most likely never become a law.

Schiller's (1995) article deals with research questions closely related to that of this study: Why do senators introduce bills if so few actually become law? Why and how do they decide to introduce bills? Which factors shape their legislative behavior? Using interviews with senators and their staff, Schiller identifies a set of factors that she deems important in influencing senators' costs-benefits calculations. Next to Schiller's research questions her dependent variable and unit of analysis in the empirical test also closely match my research design, as she is interested in the number of bills sponsored.[98] Her findings indicate that bill introduction behavior follows systematic patterns and depends on a number of factors which can be summed up as idiosyncratic factors, factors associated with the role in Congress, and constituency factors. Even though Schiller's work has a similar focus and offers some good starting points to think about individual incentives to bills sponsorship, her article is deeply rooted in the US context and rather explorative in nature instead of offering a rigorous theory that could be transferred to the context of parliamentary democracies.

Highton and Rocca (2005) also move beyond the focus on roll-calls and find strong constituency links in position taking, analyzing the example of abortion in the US. They expect the constituency connection to be stronger for non-roll-call position taking because party influence should be weaker when no direct policy consequences are to be expected. In their empirical analysis, they find that Members of Congress whose constituents have more extreme views on abortion are more likely to signal their position by sponsoring or co-sponsoring bills or by signing congressional amicus briefs. They are less likely to do this if their private opinion deviates from the constituency views.

As stated above, there is no comparable research for European parliamentary systems. Mattson (1995) takes a comparative perspective on private members' bills in Western European democracies, but he is interested in rules and procedures, not in exploring systematically the reasons for introducing bills. Hallerberg (2004: 32) gives some indirect evidence for the usage of bill sponsorship as a strategic tool to serve one's constituency in a comparative study. He shows that in systems where the personal vote is important it is more likely that restrictive procedures are imposed on the vote and that bills are voted clause-by-clause, which makes logrolls more difficult. He finds that "[s]tates with high incentives for the personal vote may lead to greater use of restrictive votes as

98 It should be mentioned here that Schiller (1995) uses OLS regression to analyze this dependent variable, which obviously has a count structure. Therefore one should be cautious with the interpretation of her results.

well as more clause-by-clause votes in an effort to discourage the MP from providing particularistic goods to her constituencies."

Transfer of the results from the US context and from the findings for other forms of legislative behavior make it seem reasonable that also the bill sponsorship behavior of French MPs can at least partly be explained by constituency and party factors: In fact, France's electoral system, where MPs are elected in single member constituencies by a two-ballot majority-plurality system, gives individual MPs high incentives to individually engage in vote-winning strategies. The MP's close connection to a certain geographic constituency helps to increase public attention in the target area: The local media is likely to cover closely the action of their local representative on the national level, which boosts the chances of the MP's legislative work being introduced to the voters.[99] Also in the direct communication with their constituents, MPs refer to their bill sponsorship behavior at the national level. On their personal websites French MPs frequently report their legislative activities.[100] While some only refer to the list of bills they authored or co-authored on the official website of the Assemblée Nationale, others offer the option to discuss the bills or to send direct feedback to the MP;[101] again others refer to their bills in speeches held in the constituency[102] or discuss

---

99 A systematic analysis of the extent to which local newspapers report on the legislative activities of the local representatives is out of the range of this study. The lack of online archives for this period for many local newspapers has also rendered a more superficial search difficult. However, I could find evidence for reports dealing with bill sponsorship activities of MPs in France. The newspaper *Dernières Nouvelles d'Alsace* reported on several proposals by the MP Armand Jung from Strasbourg, for example, concerning the proposition to pay reparation for the orphaned children of members of the *résistance* during World War II in the region Alsace-Moselle: "Armand Jung qui a déposé une proposition de loi avec deux députés mosellans visant à 'instaurer des mesures de réparation aux orphelins de déportés, à ceux de fusillés et massacrés pour faits de résistance et à ceux des patriotes résistants à l'occupation en Alsace-Moselle'" (*Dernières Nouvelles d'Alsace* 235, 6 October 2002). *Dernières Nouvelles d'Alsace* also reported on the same MP's plans to propose a ban on hunting in the suburban forests in Alsace-Moselle: "C'est pourquoi Armand Jung annonce qu'il déposera 'dès le mois de septembre, une proposition de loi plus explicite et plus complète concernant un droit de non-chasse dans les forêts péri-urbaines d'Alsace et de Moselle'" (*Dernières Nouvelles d'Alsace* 173, 23 July 2000).

100 Checking the websites of around ten percent of the current MPs revealed the following picture: While a considerable number of MPs does not have a personal website (44 percent of the sample did not report a personal website in their official biographies on the Assemblée's website http://www.assemblee-nationale.fr/qui/xml/liste_alpha.asp?legislature=13), over 90 percent of those who have a personal website wrote about their bill introduction activities, accessed on 16 March 2011.

101 http://www.michele-tabarot.fr/articles-Propositions-de-loi-54.html, accessed on 16 March 2011.

102 At the New Year's reception in 2011 the deputy Elie Aboud of the governing UMP explicitly mentioned how "extremely touched and satisfied" he was with the "success" of his bill to ban the

their motivations for drafting a bill and for their voting behavior in monthly newsletters.[103]

Also qualitative evidence from parliamentary systems suggests that bills are also targeted to an audience outside of parliament: For Belgium, van Schoor (1972) finds evidence that private members' bills serve as electoral propaganda toward constituents and clientele groups. Messerschmidt (2005: 77) speaks of private members' bills in France as means of communication with the constituency.

Many of the studies reviewed above have laid out a connection between legislative behavior of elected representatives and electoral considerations. First evidence suggests that such a connection can also be expected in parliamentary democracies, among others in France. However, the connection between constituency preferences and observed actions of representatives is not necessarily a direct one. Particularly the more recent studies emphasize the influence of both factors, the constituency and party leaders, in determining the effect on the legislative behavior of MPs. An MP's reelection is subject to the votes he receives from his constituents, but important aspects like renomination, access to party resources, or career advancement depend largely upon party leaders. The formal model developed in the subsequent section will take this double dependency of MPs into account.

4.2 A Formal Model of Private Members' Bill Introduction

The results of the research discussed above give some directions in which to search in order to answer the puzzle of bill introduction by backbenchers or opposition MPs in parliamentary democracies. In particular, I build on the findings that MPs are serving two principals: constituency (C) (represented by the constituency's median voter) and party leader (P). In the following, I will formalize the factors leading to the decision of an MP to sponsor a bill by developing a decision theoretic model. A formal model has the advantage to force clarity about the assumptions made and to ensure logical consistency by describing the mechanisms that lead to the outcome.

In the model, the MP, confronted with a certain legislative demand from his constituency, decides whether to introduce a bill or not. He makes this decision considering the fact that the party leader sanctions deviation from the party line

display of foreign flags in city halls when celebrating a civil marriage. (The speech can be found on http://www.e-aboud.fr/, accessed on 16 March 2011.

103 http://www.urvoas.org/category/lettre-info, e.g. the letter from February 2011, accessed on 16 March 2011.

in the MP's bill sponsorship activities. At the same time the MP must have in mind the median voter in his constituency whose support (in the polls or in future elections) depends on how the MP's policy signals match the constituency priorities.

This decision process is repeated t ($t = 1, \ldots, n$) times during a legislative term as often as the MP is confronted with demands for legislative activity from his constituency. Each time the MP decides whether to take up the constituency demand and signal a position on the issue at hand by sponsoring a bill and thus to risk conflict with his party leader, or whether to do nothing.

The party leader represents the official party line with the ideal point θ_P, the median voter in the MP's constituency prefers the policy position θ_C. The MP is modeled as a "Downsian" legislator, meaning that the MP chooses his position opportunistically in order to maximize his chance of reelection without pursuing policy goals on his own.

More formally, the MP can pursue one of the following strategies at any time t[104]: Either he chooses a bill with the policy position θ_{MP}, with θ_{MP} being some point in the policy space $X \subseteq \mathrm{R}^n$, or he decides to refrain from introducing ($\neg i$). By submitting a bill, the MP sends a signal to his constituency about his policy position on a certain issue. When choosing the optimal strategy, the MP has to take both the position of the party θ_P, represented by the position of the party leader, and the position of the median voter in his constituency θ_C into account. Thus his strategy is θ_{MP}: $(\theta_P,\theta_C) \rightarrow X \cup \{\neg i\}$. If the MP signals a policy position that deviates from the ideal points of his party or his constituency, he risks to be sanctioned by one of his principals. Let $F(.)$ and $G(.)$ denote the sanctioning function of the constituency and the party, respectively. I assume that $F(0) = G(0) = 0$ and that $F(.)$ increases in $||\theta_C - .||$ and $G(.)$ increases in $||\theta_P - .||$, meaning that the punishment increases with the distance of the MP's policy signal to the ideal point of the receiver of this signal.

There are two other factors influencing the utility of the MP. On the one hand there is the sanctioning potential of the voters s_C and of the party s_P (which may include how alert they are to a certain policy issue, but also how easily the median voter abandons the candidate or what possibilities and eagerness the party has to discipline their MP). On the other hand the MP has to invest the resources r to draft a bill. The costs of bill sponsorship vary between MPs, for

104 The payoffs the actors receive at time t are independent of the payoffs received in the last period. Therefore the actors will chose their strategy independent of their past decisions.

instance with the expertise of MPs or the number of staff.[105] In addition to the costs r, which are fix for an MP in each period, I introduce an additional cost factor ε_t, which takes into account costs that vary over time. Let the costs r as well as the punishment potential s_C and s_P range between 0 and 1, $0 \leq r, s_P, s_C \leq 1$. The factor ε_t is assumed to be drawn from a normal distribution with mean zero, $\varepsilon_t \sim N(0,\sigma^2)$. Finally, I assume that if an MP does not introduce his own bill on an issue, voters will perceive the MP's policy position on the issue as equivalent to that of the party.

In summary, the MP's utility from bill introduction in period t is a function of the distance between the signaled position of the MP (θ_{MP} if the MP sponsors a bill and θ_P if the MP does not signal a bill) and the ideal points of the party leader θ_P and the constituency median voter's position θ_C. In case the MP sponsors a bill, the utility is also influenced by the fixed cost factor r associated with the costs of drafting the bill and an additional random cost factor ε_t that accounts for variable costs at different points in time t. The random cost factor ε_t is assumed to follow the same distribution for all MPs.

Overall the utility of an MP is given by

$$u_t(\theta_{MP}) = \begin{cases} -F(\theta_C - \theta_{MP})s_C - G(\theta_P - \theta_{MP})s_P - r - \varepsilon_t & \text{if MP introduces } \theta_{MP} \\ -F(\theta_C - \theta_P)s_C & \text{if MP does not introduce} \end{cases} \qquad \text{I.}$$

The optimal position of the MP for introducing a bill can be found by maximizing the MP's utility u_t over θ_{MP}. Assuming quadratic loss functions to account for the negative effect of greater distance from the ideal points of the two principals of the MP, the following ideal position θ^*_{MP} for the MP can be derived:

$$\frac{\partial u}{\partial \theta_{MP}} = 2\left(\theta_C - \theta^*_{MP}\right)s_C + 2\left(\theta_P - \theta^*_{MP}\right)s_P = 0 \qquad \text{II.}$$

Hence, $\theta^*_{MP} = \frac{s_C}{s_C + s_P}\theta_C + \frac{s_P}{s_C + s_P}\theta_P$, that is, the optimal position that the MP should signal to his constituency and his party is a compromise between the ideal points of these two actors, weighted by their relative sanctioning potential. When the MP decides not to introduce a bill, his utility is independent of θ_{MP}. Consequently, the optimal position of a bill is given by

[105] All factors in the model differ (at least potentially) between MPs. For the ease of presentation I refrain from using an index i on all variables.

$$\theta_{MP}^{*} = \begin{cases} \frac{s_C}{s_C + s_P}\theta_C + \frac{s_P}{s_C + s_P}\theta_P & \text{if MP introduces a bill} \\ x \in \square & \text{if MP does not introduce} \end{cases} \qquad \text{III.}$$

The strategy to sponsor a bill is dominant if the utility of introducing a bill with the optimal position θ_{MP} is higher than the utility from not introducing, hence if $u_t(\theta_{MP}^{*}) \geq u(\neg i)$. In the following, I assume that $\theta_C = 0$ and that θ_P lies on the unit interval [0,1]. This eases the presentation of results without loss of generality. Hence the MP will sponsor a bill if:

$$-\theta_{MP}^{*2} s_C - \left(\theta_P - \theta_{MP}^{*}\right)^2 s_P - r - \varepsilon_t \geq -\theta_P^2 s_C \qquad \text{IV.}$$

After simplifying this inequality one gets the following result for the average maximum level of individual costs for drafting a bill r^* for which it would still be worth introducing a bill, rather than refraining from doing anything:

$$r^{*} = \frac{s_C^2}{s_C + s_P}\theta_P^2 \qquad \text{V.}$$

Equation V indicates the level of r^* for which it is just as good to introduce a bill at time t as not to introduce a bill. An MP will therefore introduce a bill at time t if his personal costs of drafting a bill r are less-than-or-equal-to the maximum level of costs r^* which provides at least as much utility as not introducing a bill. A higher level of s_C, that is, a higher sanctioning potential of the constituency, leads to a higher maximum level of r^* an MP is willing to invest. The utility from introducing a bill signaling a diverging position increases also the larger the policy distance between constituency and party. Hence, a higher level of θ_P increases the probability that an MP will introduce a bill. When party and constituency have the same position, hence if $\theta_P = \theta_C = 0$, an MP would never introduce a bill to signal divergence from the party line, unless the bill were costless.

Figure 10 Level of r^* for which the Utility of Introducing Exceeds the Utility of Refraining in Dependence of s_P at Different Levels of s_C.

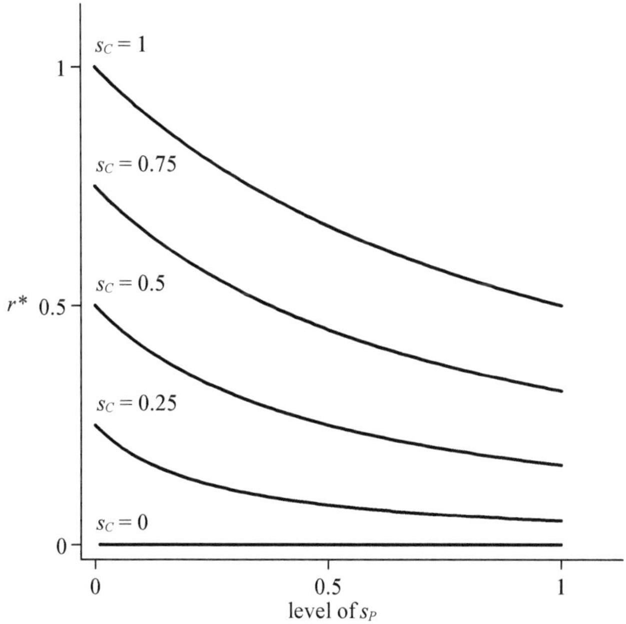

Note: The party position and the random error are fixed at $\theta_P = 1$ and $\varepsilon = 0$.

Without the random costs factor ε_t, an MP would introduce a bill at all times t if he faces an individual cost level lower than the maximum costs he would be willing to pay given the sanctioning potential of party and constituency ($r \leq r^*$). An MP with individual costs exceeding the maximum cost level ($r > r^*$) would never introduce a bill. Considering the random costs factor ε_t leads to a more nuanced picture: Figure 11 shows the distribution of the overall costs that an MP would be willing to pay given the maximum cost level r^* (in this example $r^* = 0.5$) and the normally distributed random cost factor ε_t. The grey colored area indicates the probability that for a given individual cost level r an MP will introduce a bill. In case a), where the individual cost level equals the maximum costs at which bill introduction is better than refraining from bill sponsorship, the MP will introduce a bill half the time. If r is considerably larger than r^* as in case b), the MP will only rarely introduce a bill. In case c), where bill introduction is fairly cheap for an MP, he will at almost all occasions introduce a bill.

Figure 11 Probability of Bill Introduction ($r \leq r^* + \varepsilon_t$)

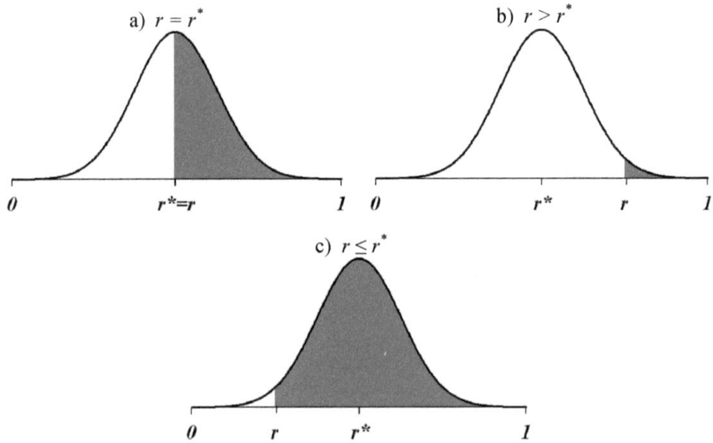

In the model outlined above, an MP's decision to introduce legislation depends on the sanctioning potential and the relative distance between the positions of the constituency and the party, as well as on the resources needed to draft the bill. The following hypotheses can thus be derived from the model:

> *Hypothesis 1* The higher the party's sanctioning potential, the fewer bills diverging from the party line the MP will introduce on average.

The connection between r^* and the sanctioning potential of party and constituency is depicted in Figure 10, in which one can already see that a higher sanctioning potential of the party leads to a lower r^* and consequently on average to fewer bills. This connection can also be shown formally using comparative statics for s_P:

$$\frac{\partial r^*}{\partial s_P} = -\frac{s_C^2 \theta_P^2}{\left(s_C + s_P\right)^2} < 0 \qquad \text{VI.}$$

Hypothesis 2 The higher the voters' sanctioning potential, the more bills an MP will introduce all else equal.

Again this relationship is obvious from the comparative statics:

$$\frac{\partial r^*}{\partial s_C} = \frac{s_C \theta_P^2 \left(s_C + 2s_P\right)}{\left(s_C + s_P\right)^2} > 0 \qquad \text{VII.}$$

Hypothesis 3 The higher the individual costs of introducing bills, the fewer bills an MP will introduce.

Given r^* does not change, a higher individual cost level r makes bill introduction less likely, as shown in Figure 11.

Hypothesis 4 The larger the gap between the party's and the constituency's ideal policy position, the more bills an MP will introduce.

As the comparative statics show, an increase in the distance between party and constituency is strictly related to an increasing preparedness to invest more resources:

$$\frac{\partial r^*}{\partial \theta_P} = \frac{2s_C \theta_P}{\left(s_C + s_P\right)^2} > 0 \qquad \text{VIII.}$$

4.3 Empirical Evidence from the French Assemblée Nationale

In order to test the hypotheses empirically, the central concepts, such as the costs of a bill and the sanctioning potential of voters and parties, have to be operationalized. In the following, I will derive empirical implications of the model specifically for the French context, with a focus on the period 1997-2002. The 577 MPs of the French Assemblée Nationale are elected in majority runoff elections in single member districts. As each MP from one party has to compete for the votes of a different subsample of the national electorate, it is likely that all MPs want to appeal to median voters with different positions. Hence, signaling deviation from the party line seems per se a good strategy.

4.3.1 Data and Measurements

In order to test the hypotheses derived above empirically, I confront the theory with data on legislation in France during the 11th legislative period (1997-2002). All the data has been collected from official government resources, such as the *journal officiel* (the official gazette of the French Republic), official biographies of the parliamentarians and other information from the Website of the Assemblée Nationale, or population census data. The dependent variables are measured as count data, namely the number of bills introduced by the individual member of the French Assemblée Nationale. In addition to taking the *total number of bills sponsored*, I distinguish between three types of bills: First, I count all bills that were introduced by a single MP individually. *Single-authored bills* without anyone co-signing them are the most likely to serve the purpose of taking up constituency interests and sending policy signals on issues that are ignored by the national party or on which the MP wants to be distinguished from the party line. For these bills the model outlined above should apply best. Second, there are *bills supported by the parliamentary party group*, which serve a different purpose. They can be understood as a service to the party that wants to signal policy positions to the national audience or to potential coalition partners. Between these two categories lies the third type: *bills authored or supported by at least two MPs*. Such multi-authored bills can be the result of cooperation between MPs with similar constituency interests or, for instance, policy signals of a faction within a party group. Information on the bills was extracted from various *journaux officiels*[106] between 1997 and 2002.[107]

4.3.2 Applying the Theoretical Model to France: Independent Variables

The sanctioning potential of the party s_P depends on different factors outlined below. The *government status* of a party is likely to play a prominent role in the sanctioning potential of a party. On the one hand government parties can be expected to be interested in being perceived as a cohesive group. Especially on issues on which government has already taken position, deviating MPs are likely to be punished. On the other hand government parties also have more resources

---

106 http://www.legifrance.gouv.fr/

107 The legislative data comes from the data set compiled in the project "Comparative Legislation" headed by Thomas Bräuninger (DFG grant BR 1851/3). Additional information on co-sponsors and group support was coded using the information in the online dossiers for the specific legislation: http://www.assemblee-nationale.fr/11/documents/index-proposition.asp, accessed on 16 December 2010.

than opposition parties to buy the support (or at least abstinence from open dissent) of their party members by offering prospects for higher office or policy deals favorable for an MP's constituency. Overall signaling dissent should be easier for opposition MPs.

The *internal organization of the party groups* determines the power and also the incentive of a party group to punish deviating members. A party group that has the goal to be perceived as a unitary actor is more likely to have the means and the intention to punish deviating members than a party group that is composed of independents and members of small parties who only found together in order to benefit from the advantages of being organized in a party group.[108] Whereas the previous assumption stated that government parties should be more interested in keeping close ranks, parties can be expected to differ independently of their government status in the display of party discipline. There are enormous differences in the role and organization of the parliamentary party groups. In the period under study (1997-2002) three party groups supported government: The Socialists, the Communists, and the group Radical, Citoyen, Vert (RCV). Whereas the communists had just recently abandoned the Stalinist principle of "democratic centralism" (Knapp and Wright 2001: 177) but still put much emphasis on the "necessary united action" in their declaration, the declaration of the RCV party group – a partnership of convenience made up of small left and green parties and left-wing independents – only consisted of four phrases stating that members of this group take no directives and are only responsible to their conscience.[109] The communist party group and the RCV are certainly the most extremes on the continuum from strict organization and loose cooperation. However, also the other party groups can be classified as more or less strong and unified: For the party groups of the Socialists, Communists, and RPR, usually just one candidate is chosen for the presidency of the group by the external party organization, who is then confirmed through vote by the group members; in the other party groups, usually (competitive) elections within the group take place (Thiébault and Dolez 2000: 61). Differences can also be observed with regard to voting, where the Socialist and Communist groups practice a disciplined vote,

---

[108] In France during the period studied here, at least 20 MPs were required to form a parliamentary party group (Thiébault and Dolez 2000: 58). Before 1988, even 30 MPs were needed to constitute a parliamentary party group (Thiébault and Dolez 2000: 58). In 2009 the minimum number was reduced to 15 (Assemblée Nationale 2009: 149). To organize as a party group has advantages concerning, for instance, the distribution of membership in committees and allocation of time for speeches. The presidents of the parliamentary party groups also participate in setting the order of the day in the "conference of presidents" (Thiébault and Dolez 2000: 60).

[109] http://www.assemblee-nationale.fr/11/qui/declarations-groupes.asp, accessed on 16 December 2010.

the RPR group decides issue by issue, while the other groups have a tradition of freedom of voting (Thiébault and Dolez 2000: 62-63). The RPR, the Socialist, and the Communist groups also restrict individual rights, such as submitting private members' bills, resolutions, or amendments, or asking oral and written questions. Members of these groups are supposed to obtain approval by the party group first (Thiébault and Dolez 2000: 63).

Also the *electoral success (marginality)* of an MP is likely to influence the potential to keep the MP under party group control. The more electorally successful an MP, the more independent he is expected to be from his party group. In electoral campaigns he will depend less on the support of national party big shots, his renomination is more likely, and he can always argue that he speaks for a considerable number of voters. This higher level of independence reduces the level of the party's sanctioning potential.[110]

On a similar basis the *accumulation of mandates* that is possible and frequent in France (Blais 2006) can produce strong local "barons" who are relatively independent of the national party. Holding a *special post* within parliament or within the party again increases the MP's independence of the national party and makes sanctioning for deviating legislative behavior more difficult.

The sanctioning potential of the constituency s_C is more difficult to translate into empirically measureable concepts. The following operationalizations are the best solution with the data available.

If a *third party* competed in the second round of the previous election, this is likely to increase the potential to sanction a candidate for the constituency. Usually alliances form in the second round of elections so that only the strongest candidates of the left and the right compete against each other. Independent candidates, or rivals from the same ideological camp with whom no strategic alliance was built (in 1997 especially candidates of the extreme right-wing party Front National), could nevertheless run for the second round. Hence, a third party candidate is not a tool in the hand of the electorate to control their MP, but it puts the MP in a more complex strategic environment. An MP of the left, who won against two right-wing candidates, should make an extra effort to please his

[110] This line of reasoning, however, rather contradicts the findings in the US context where MPs from marginal districts are found to deviate more often from the party line in roll-calls (compare e.g. MacRae 1952 who first developed the "marginality hypotheses" stating that electoral insecurity leads to a closer connection to the constituency or Pesonen 1963). Yet, deviation in parliamentary votes does not necessarily mean better representation. Some authors (e.g. Jones 1973, Fiorina 1973) doubt that MPs from marginal districts represent their constituency better. Whether the independence of the party or the pressure to do something for the constituency is stronger, is an empirical question. Generally partisan pressure in the French context is expected to be higher than in the United States.

constituency, since a united right-wing could be a serious challenge in the next election. A candidate of the right, who won against a left and a right competitor, might fear to lose ground in the next election if he does not build up a good reputation in the constituency, since the voters have two potential alternatives. Sulkin (2005) finds evidence that members of the US Congress are more successful in elections if they use speeches or bill sponsorship to signal policy interest on issues that their challengers brought up in campaigns. A similar effect could be expected especially for MPs with third party challengers in France.

In order to be able to control the activities of the constituency MP, voters need information on the MP's activities. While the MP will take care of spreading positive news of his legislative activities at least during the electoral campaign in the constituency, more objective coverage of the MP's activities can be expected from the *local press.* When a lot of voters are informed about an MP's activities, the MP is more likely to be responsive to the constituency's demands. Consequently a strong local press should increase the sanctioning potential of the constituency.[111]

Also the *age* of an MP is likely to play a role in the potential to sanction an MP for (in)activity or (non)responsive activities: The younger an MP, the more likely it is that he has still a lot of career ambitions and tries to please his constituency. Older MPs who come closer to retirement age might put less effort in winning votes for their reelection. However, age as a proxy of career ambition could also influence the party's sanctioning potential as it usually controls the career paths. Therefore young MPs could be careful not to irritate the party leaders by moving too far off the party line. Which effect will dominate is an empirical question.

While influencing the sanctioning potential of the party, *marginality* of the electoral district might also have a countervailing effect on the sanctioning potential of the constituency. The closer the results of the previous election, the more important it is for an MP to send an optimal policy signal to the constituency. In contrast, an MP who won by a large margin in the previous election can more easily accept losing some votes due to a biased signal of his position without risking his reelection chances.

Costs of a bill ***r*** will be operationalized as follows: MPs with a *judicial background* are expected to have lower average costs per bill because of their

111 Unfortunately, I do not have constituency level information on the impact of the local press. However, the EPIQ studies show that there is a significant gap between readers of local newspapers in the Île-de-France and the rest of France. The 2006/2007 study (which provides the oldest results reported online) reports that only 17 percent of the inhabitants of the Île-de-France read a regional newspaper, whereas more than 39 percent of the rest of France do so. The results of the study can be found on http://www.audipresse.fr/node.php?id=905, accessed on 1 April 2011.

expertise with legislative texts. Expertise will also be built up with *past experience* in the Assemblée Nationale. MPs who have served longer in the Assemblée Nationale have to invest less on average in preparing a bill. The positive effect of the *accumulation of offices* mentioned above on the number of bills introduced should be reinforced by the effect of holding several offices on the relative costs of a bill: While all MPs receive a fixed amount of money to employ up to five parliamentary assistants,[112] MPs with additional local mandates are likely to have more staff and experts for local issues at their disposal. These MPs also gain experience with legislation from their lower level electoral office. All this should add to lower costs per unit for MPs with multiple offices. On the same line of reasoning, MPs with a *special post* dispose of higher resources.

$|\boldsymbol{\theta_P} - \boldsymbol{\theta_C}|$, which reflects the distance between the positions of party and constituency,[113] would be best measured using information on the left-right positions of party and constituency. As this data is not available, alternative measures have to be considered. Differences in socio-economic indicators for different constituencies could be taken as a proxy for positional differences. Alternatively, a simple dummy variable can distinguish between MPs from the French mainland and the overseas territories, which differ in socio-economic conditions, climate, culture, and many other factors.[114]

Some of the empirical indicators potentially relate to more than one of the theoretical concepts. Table 20 summarizes the expected relationship between the indicators and the theoretical concepts and presents the overall expected effect as well as the operationalization of the variables.

Signaling interest for constituency voters' interests and a distinct position from the party line can be done in a number of ways, bill sponsorship being just one option. Less costly alternatives in order to gain a personal vote could be available in small constituencies where the MP can more easily foster direct contact with his voters. Therefore I use the constituency size as a control variable in the subsequent analyses. I also control for whether the MP served the whole term to see if leaving parliament during a term has any systematic consequences for bill sponsorship.

---

112 http://www.assemblee-nationale.fr/connaissance/fiches_synthese/fiche_83.asp, accessed on 31 March 2011.

113 The distance between party and constituency is $|\theta_P - \theta_C|$. As $\theta_C = 0$ by definition and $\theta_P \geq 0$ the distance is given by θ_P.

114 A measure considering the absolute deviation from the party median constituency on several socio-economic factors has been tested. Little evidence for an effect was found, however, and several cases were lost due to missing data. Therefore only the more conservative results using the "overseas territories" dummy are reported.

Table 20 Relationship of Variables with Theoretical Concepts and Expected Effects on Number of Bills Introduced

Variables	Effect on s_P, s_C, r, θ_P	Overall exp. effect on # of bills	Operationalization
Opposition	s_P –	+	Dummy variable: 1 if MP's party is in opposition, 0 otherwise
Cohesion	s_P +	–	Dummy variable: 1 if party group is cohesive (Socialist, Communist, and RPR group), 0 otherwise
Third party	s_C +	+	Dummy variable: 1 if third party entered 2nd round of elections, 0 otherwise
Île-de-France (Press Coverage)	s_C –	–	Dummy variable: 1 if MP's constituency belongs to Île-de-France, 0 otherwise
Judicial Experience	r –	+	Dummy variable: 1 if MP has a judicial background, 0 otherwise
Past Legislative Experience	r –	+	Dummy variable: 1 if MP has served in the Assemblée Nationale before, 0 otherwise
Overseas Constituency	θ_P +	+	Dummy variable: 1 if MP's constituency is not on the French mainland, 0 otherwise
Age	s_P –, s_C –	?	Age in years of MP at the beginning of the legislative period in 1997
Accumulation	s_P –, r –	+	Number of elected offices an MP holds in addition to the national mandate
Marginality	s_P +, s_C +	?	Result winner minus result of the strongest competitor in the 1997 elections

Special Post	s_P-, $r-$	+	Dummy variable: 1 if MP holds a special post in parliament or party[115], 0 otherwise

For the independent variables the following sources were used: First, biographic information of the parliamentarians, which comes from the official biographies on the website of the Assemblée Nationale.[116] Second, from the same website, the official results in the constituencies.[117] Third, constituency data, which stems from the 1999 census by the French national institute of statistics.[118] Table 24 in the Appendix to this chapter gives an overview over the distribution of all variables.

4.3.3 Bill Introduction in the French Assemblée Nationale

Having described the data used for the empirical testing of the model, I will now give some more background information on the circumstances of the period under observation and describe the bill introduction behavior of parliamentarians in this particular period, 1997-2002 more closely.

The results of the 1997 French national elections led to a victory of the left-wing parties. Table 21 gives an overview of the seat distribution after the elections. Just one day after the election the Socialist Lionel Jospin was nominated *premier ministre* by the conservative president Jacques Chirac. The left-wing government was formed two days later by the *gauche plurielle*, encompassing all left-wing parties plus the green party in government. These parties had already formed a pre-electoral alliance, in which all left parties would support the strongest left-wing candidate of the first round in the second round. The situation of *cohabitation* lasted for the whole five years of the legislative period. However, there were 18 cabinet reshuffles. As ministers and secretaries of state are not allowed to keep their seat in the Assemblée Nationale due to the incompatibility of parliamentary mandate and government function (article 23 of the constitution), the nomination of an MP into cabinet also affects the composition of par-

115 I define the following positions as "special post": Presidents and vice-presidents of the parliamentary committees, president of the Assemblée Nationale, heads of the parliamentary party groups, presidents and secretary-generals of the political parties.

116 http://www.assemblee-nationale.fr/11/qui/index.asp, accessed on 5 July 2007. I would like to thank the student assistants Katrin Kirschmann and Külvi Noor who helped collecting the data.

117 http://www.assemblee-nationale.fr/elections/circ97-2/, accessed on 22 November 2007.

118 http://www.webcommerce.insee.fr/fiche-produit.php?id_produit=599, accessed on 26 September 2007.

liament as a replacement is elected in by-elections. Overall, 71 of the 577 MPs were replaced between 1997 and 2002 for this and for other reasons, such as annulment of the election in a constituency, election as senator, or even death.

The legislative records of the individual deputies differ widely: Whereas almost half of the 577 deputies did not even introduce a single bill, the most active deputy is author of 44 bills. Altogether, the 577 originally elected deputies introduced 1313 bills (compare Table 25 in the Appendix to this chapter for more details).[119]

Table 21 Seats Gained in the 1997 Assemblée Nationale Elections by Party Group

Parliamentary Majority	Seats
Socialiste	250
Communiste	36
Radical, Citoyen et Vert	33
Total Seats Government	319
Opposition Groups	Seats
Rassemblement pour la République	140
UDF	113
Non inscrits	5
Total Seats Opposition	258
Total Seats	577

Note: This table describes the situation right after the national elections. In 1998, a new group "Démocratie libérale et indépendants" was formed primarily of former UDF members.

[119] As mentioned above, due to fluctuations in parliament, another 71 deputies were elected in by-elections to replace parliamentarians who dropped out during the legislative period. Together, these 71 replacements introduced another 63 bills. However, they are omitted from the analysis as the data set is incomplete for the replacements. Also, the 19 MPs who joined the government right from the beginning and therefore never had the chance to introduce a private members' bill were excluded from the analysis. In addition, seven of the 22 deputies from the French overseas departments and territories had to be omitted due to missing data. As a result, the statistical analyses are conducted for 551 MPs.

The first *proposition de loi* (private members' bill) was introduced only two weeks after the second round of the election by Jean Louis Masson.[120] The last bill was still introduced only one week before the end of the legislative period. The most active parliamentarian, Yves Nicolin, introduced his first bill after more than a year. Of his 44 bills, not a single one was adopted.

Cooperation between the government and opposition MPs on bill introduction was almost non-existent: Only one bill was introduced by an MP from the government camp together with an opposition MP. The bill dealt with a regional matter, concerning an issue of the MPs' *départements* Alsace and Moselle during the Second World War.

The success rate of opposition bills lies below one percent. Only seven out of 895 bills introduced by the opposition were finally adopted. All of these bills were amended before finding a majority in parliament. These bills also have in common that their authors explicitly refer to their non-partisan character and the necessity to find a consensual solution.[121] The content of the bills deals with issues/groups of people that are not well suited for party dispute, such as orphans, abused children, child adoption, disabled people (two bills), and injured soldiers. The odd one out deals with housing subsidies, but still, this bill also targets a weak socio-economic group.

Bills originating from government MPs have a significantly higher success rate. Around ten percent of the bills introduced by MPs belonging to one of the

---

[120] Masson was forced to realize his legislative agenda very fast as he was facing the threat of annulment of the election from the very beginning. Right after the election, there were investigations about irregularities in his campaign financing. Before the *conseil constitutionnel* annulated his election about half a year later and excluded him from competing in elections for one year, Masson had introduced a total of twelve bills.

[121] Two of the seven successful bills introduced by opposition MPs are non-partisan *par excellence*: Bill number 412 and bill number 1797 originate from the "parlement des enfants". Each year one class from one school in each constituency sends a delegate to the parliament of children. The children are ten or eleven years old. In their schools they can prepare a bill that they hand in beforehand and, on acceptance, can later present in the parliament of children. A jury selects ten bills, which the delegates discuss in committees before they put the top three bills on the agenda for the public session. Finally they take a vote on these bills. The winning bill of the parliament of children is then usually taken up by the MP of the sponsoring school's constituency and indeed introduced to the *Assemblée Nationale*. (For more information on the parliament of children, see http://www.parlementdesenfants.fr/, accessed on 6 April 2011). Also government MPs introduced bills that originate from the parliament of children, namely bill number 1069 and bill number 3247. All four children bills were adopted (with amendments) by parliament. Consequently four of the 52 successful parliamentary bills originate from this truly non-partisan source. The four bills deal with the detection of child abuse, the interdiction to buy school furniture from countries with child labor, the improvement of the situation of orphans, and an amelioration of the possibilities of children to stay in touch with their imprisoned parents.

three parliamentary party groups supporting government succeed. Yet even though government party bills are adopted much more frequently than opposition bills, still nine out of ten bills fail. A closer look at the bills from the government camp reveals a more nuanced picture of whose bills become law: The success rate of Socialist MPs, the largest parliamentary party group supporting government, lies at above 26 percent, whereas bills originating from the communist party group or the RCV party group are only rarely successful (four and six percent respectively). Duhamel and Parodi (1988) argue that during cohabitation, as in the period considered here, the government sometimes uses private members to submit government bills in order to avoid the obligatory review by the Council of State for government bills. This procedure can probably account for at least some of the successful bills.

Almost 60 percent of the overall 52 successful bills originate from socialists. The three Socialists Jean le Garrec, Jean-Marc Ayrault, and Laurent Fabius sign responsible for more than half of the successful socialist bills (16 out of 31). These three MPs also show the most impressive individual legislative records. Jean-Marc Ayrault, president of the parliamentary group of the governing Socialists, was the most successful parliamentarian in absolute numbers: Nine of the 22 bills he sponsored were adopted.[122] His colleague in the Socialist party group, Jean Le Garrec, who had occupied several government posts in earlier Socialist governments, has a similarly impressive record with all five bills he (co-)authored being adopted.[123] Laurent Fabius, former Socialist prime minister, who was president of the Assemblée Nationale and later became Minister of Economy, Finance, and Industry during the period studied here, sponsored four (out of six) successful bills. Overall, the success rate of bills from MPs with leading positions within the Socialist party group is above 45 percent.

These descriptive statistics of the success rate of bills confirms the picture described above: Parliamentary bills are rarely successful with the important exception of bills from the biggest party group supporting government. Successful opposition bills are consensual in nature. Although they are always amended before their adoption, they are likely to arouse positive public attention. However, they are neither very useful as a signal of a party's policy difference from another party on the party level, nor as a signal of a deviating position from one's own party on the individual level. In that they are no typical sample of the bills introduced to parliament. A large proportion of the bills MPs draft do not attempt consensual policy change, but seek to attract the attention of the voters

122 19 of the 22 bills were supported by the entire party group, the other three at least by several other members of the party group.

123 Four out of five of these bills were supported by the Socialist party group, the other one supported by at least parts of the group. Two of the bills were co-authored with Jean-Marc Ayrault.

and try to send policy signals. Many bills actually refer directly to the geographic constituency of their author(s), such as bill number 20, which demands financing the high-speed train connection Rhin-Rhône; bill number 1298, which is concerned with the organization of trade unions in Corsica; or bill number 1015, which seeks to create a région "Savoie". A nice example of reference to the constituency voters is also bill number 3693, in which the author asks to "reestablish the dignity" of the voters in the French Antilles and Guyana. Other private members' bills do not refer to the geographic constituency, but are still likely to provide publicity, such as bill number 3274, in which the author asks to store the bank notes and coins of the French Franc in order to be able to replace the Euro within days in case the European currency fails.

The theoretical model outline above will not apply to all bills equally well. Therefore, in order to test the theoretical model, I distinguish between a) bills that find the support of the party group as a whole, b) bills that are not supported by the party group as a whole, but by at least one other or more MPs (generally from the respective MP's own party group), and c) bills that are introduced individually by single MPs. The first kind of bill signals individual activity, possibly directed against the party line as modeled above. The second category is less clear. Co-sponsorship could be the result of cooperation due to similar situations in two or more MPs' constituencies but also because the cooperating MPs belong to the same intraparty faction or because they have complementary expertise. The last category can be understood as a service to the party and as a signal of agreeing with the party's position.

Table 22 gives an overview over how frequently the different types of bills were used by MPs of the government and opposition camp. The aggregate data already indicates support for the hypothesized connection between government status and the usage of single-authored bills. However, there is also a large variation between individual MPs that I analyze in the remainder of this chapter.

Table 22 Bills by Bill Type and Government Status

	Total	Single-authored	Co-authored (non-group)	Group supported
Gov. Majority	417	71	109	237
Mixed	1		1	0
Opposition	895	443	410	42
Total	1313	514	520	279

4.3.4 Regression Model

Several models have been developed to deal specifically with count data, most prominently the Poisson regression model. As already discussed in more detail in the previous chapters, the *negative binomial regression model* (NBRM) offers an alternative to the Poisson regression model. Whereas both have the same mean structure, the variance equations of the two models differ. In addition to accounting for observed heterogeneity as does the latter, the NBRM also accounts for unobserved heterogeneity by introducing an error term (Long and Freese 2006: 372). Thus, the NBRM fits better when there is overdispersion, which means that the conditional variance is larger than the conditional mean. For the data at hand, statistical tests suggest that the NBRM is the appropriate model. In fact, Figure 12 indicates that it fits the data quite well. The results of these estimates are presented in Table 23.

4.3.5 Empirical Results

Overdispersion is present in all four models presented in Table 23; α is significantly larger than 1 in all models at the 1 percent level. Therefore using a NBRM is clearly preferred over a Poisson regression model.[124] All four models also fit the data better than a constant only model as indicated by the Wald χ^2 test and the pseudo R^2. To account for the fact that not all parliamentarians stayed in parliament over the whole period, I considered the days in parliament as exposure time in all count models.

In the first negative binomial regression model I examine whether the theoretical model outlined above can explain the *total number of bills* introduced by an MP. Most variables have the expected sign and are statistically significant. Opposition MPs sponsor more bills on average. Being a member of a more cohesive party group reduces the number of bills introduced. These indicators of party group sanctioning potential are highly significant at the one percent level. The evidence for the constituency sanctioning potential is mixed: As expected, the existence of a third party competitor in the second round of the election increases the number of bills introduced on average. While this indicator is marginally significant at the ten percent level, the second indicator "Île-de-France",

---

[124] Zero-inflated negative binomial regression fits the data just as well. However, there should be two theoretically distinct mechanisms that lead to the introduction of zero bills in order to justify such a model. As I cannot think of a theoretical reason that generally excludes some group of representatives from introducing bill, I chose the more parsimonious simple negative binomial regression model.

which is supposed to be an indicator of the spread of the local press and therefore of information about the activities of the constituency's MP, has a positive instead of the expected negative sign and fails any conventional level of significance.

Figure 12 Observed Number of Bills vs. Prediction of Negative Binomial Regression Model

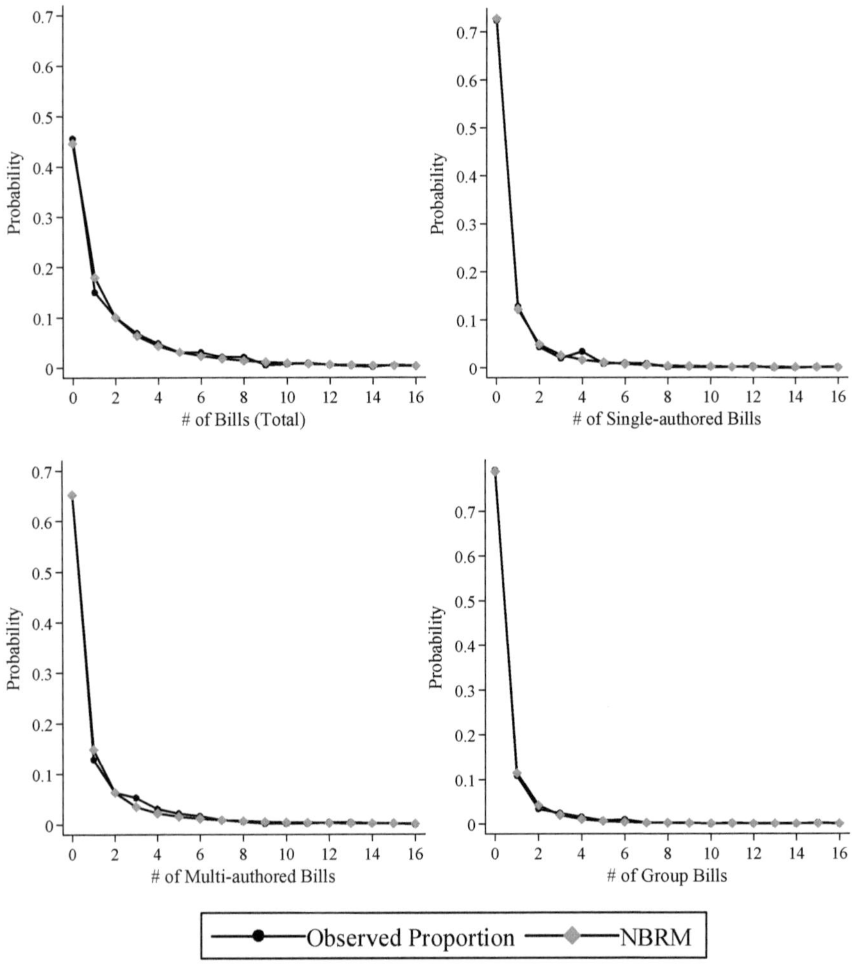

Table 23 Results of Negative Binomial Regression Models for Bill Sponsorship

	(1) All bills	(2) Single-authored	(3) Co-authored (non-group)	(4) Group supported
Party Group Sanctioning Potential				
Opposition	1.055***	2.019***	1.651***	-0.805***
	(0.17)	(0.28)	(0.22)	(0.26)
Cohesion	-0.678***	-0.904***	-1.289***	0.844**
	(0.17)	(0.23)	(0.20)	(0.34)
Constituency Sanctioning Potential				
Third party	0.429**	0.636**	0.347	0.253
	(0.21)	(0.27)	(0.26)	(0.36)
Île-de-France	0.071	0.235	0.111	0.097
	(0.17)	(0.29)	(0.22)	(0.25)
Costs				
Judicial Experience	0.299	0.758**	0.485*	-0.100
	(0.20)	(0.32)	(0.26)	(0.33)
Several LPs	0.352**	0.466	0.304	0.480*
	(0.18)	(0.29)	(0.24)	(0.27)
Distance btw. Positions				
Overseas Const.	-0.045	0.525	0.396	-0.963
	(0.29)	(0.54)	(0.48)	(0.67)
Mixed Indicators				
Age	-0.020**	-0.047***	-0.010	-0.010
	(0.01)	(0.01)	(0.01)	(0.02)
Accumulation	0.033	0.195**	0.137	-0.095
	(0.07)	(0.10)	(0.10)	(0.10)
Electoral Margin	1.926***	1.817**	0.573	1.966***
	(0.41)	(0.73)	(0.50)	(0.53)
Special Post	0.823***	0.286	0.796***	1.255***
	(0.19)	(0.35)	(0.23)	(0.25)

Controls				
Constituency Size	0.100^{**} (0.04)	0.063 (0.06)	0.164^{***} (0.06)	0.031 (0.06)
Early End	0.977^{***} (0.33)	1.691^{***} (0.57)	0.779^{***} (0.28)	0.605 (0.37)
Constant	-7.742^{***} (0.67)	-8.041^{***} (0.87)	-9.784^{***} (0.90)	-9.378^{***} (1.18)
α	1.728^{***}	2.879^{***}	1.885^{***}	3.300^{***}
Pseudo R^2	0.0718	0.1253	0.1285	0.0810
Wald $\chi^2(13)$	185.52^{***}	200.99^{***}	242.52^{***}	87.23^{***}
N	551	551	551	545[125]

Note: Days in parliament as exposure time; * significant at 10 percent ** at 5 percent *** at 1 percent; robust standard errors in parentheses

The measures for the individual cost level of drafting a bill both have the expected sign. However, only the effect of having past experience in the Assemblée Nationale is significant (at the 5 percent level). From the theoretical model also clear predictions for the effect of the distance between the position of the national party and the constituency median could be derived. In lack of positional data, I used an indicator whether an MP represents an overseas constituency. These constituencies should have special concerns which are not necessarily in the focus of the national parties. The sign indicates that MPs from overseas departments and territories are less active sponsoring bills. Yet, this effect is not statistically significant.[126]

For some indicators it could not be clearly decided whether they implied a higher constituency or party sanctioning potential. Among them was the age of

---

125 The six independent MPs who never belonged to a party group were excluded from the analysis of group supported bills.

126 As an alternative proxy for positional differences I constructed an index using information on the socio-economic situation of a constituency. However, the sum of the (absolute) deviation of the constituency's socio-economic situation (regarding, unemployment rate, proportion of foreigners, GDP (on the departmental level), and proportion of people employed in the tertiary sector) from the party average does not have a significant effect either. I decided to report the results using the simpler indicator for overseas constituencies, because with the socio-economic data some cases had to be dropped due to missing data. Additionally, the reported results are more conservative.

an MP. While young MPs are expected to strive for reelection by the constituency and for a positive relationship with the party for their career advancement, older MPs should be able to act more freely from both pressures. The empirical results show that the low sanctioning from both sides leads to lower bill sponsorship activity of older MPs, whereas the younger MPs introduce more bills on average. The overall number of accumulated political posts does not significantly influence the overall number of bills. The electoral margin has a significant positive effect: The more clearly an MP won over the closest competitor, the more bills he introduces on average. Having a special post within parliament or in the party leads to a significantly higher total number of bills sponsored.

The two control variables have statistically significant effects: MPs representing larger constituencies more frequently rely on bill sponsorship. The MPs who left parliament during the term are systematically distinct from the other MPs concerning their bill sponsorship behavior when controlling for the duration of mandate. MPs who leave the parliament early sponsor more bills on average.

While there is some evidence for the empirical implications of the theoretical model developed above when using the total number of bills as dependent variable, it makes sense to disaggregate the dependent variable. The theoretical model explains the mechanisms leading to the usage of bills as tools for distinction from the party line. However, not all bills will seek this goal. As we have seen in the previous chapters, bills can also serve the goal to signal positions to the voters. Therefore a distinction of different kinds of bills seems appropriate. Bills which are supported by the whole party group should reflect the official party line and should consequently follow different mechanisms. Bills introduced by individual MPs without the support of others are especially suited for signaling a position diverging from the official party line. For these bills the expected mechanisms should be best visible. The third kind of bills that can be distinguished, are bills sponsored or at least supported by several MPs from the same party group but not by the entire group. These bills could signal deviation from the official party line just as single-authored bills. A reason to co-sponsor could be identical interests of MPs who are subject to the same constituency pressures to diverge from the party line. In these cases the theoretical model developed in this chapter should apply as well. Yet, also other mechanisms could apply if the bill is used as a policy signal of a faction within the party group for instance.[127]

[127] An interesting next step could be the analysis of the co-sponsorship networks of French MPs to detect which factors dominate cooperation within party groups. Among others these might be geographic origin, ideological similarities between constituents, or belonging to the same faction within a party group.

Model 2 in Table 23 shows the effect of the same set of independent variables already used in model 1 on the number of *single-authored bills* submitted by an MP. The results are quite similar to the results of model 1. The effects all have the same sign with the exception of the "overseas constituency" variable. While the coefficient has a negative sign for the total number of bills, it indicates a positive relationship with single-authored bills. However, the effect is statistically insignificant in all models.

Two additional variables expected to positively influence the submission of bills in the theoretical model are now statistically significant: MPs with judicial experience sponsor more single-authored bills on average, just as MPs who accumulated more posts are more active authors of individually sponsored bills. Also the effect sizes are more pronounced for most variables. Exceptions are the "electoral margin" variable, and the "special post" variable, which even loses its statistical significance, just as the control variable constituency size. The variable controlling for past legislative experience just fails the ten percent significance level.

On average members of an opposition party group sponsor more than seven times as many single-authored bills as government MPs everything else equal.[128] Members of more cohesive groups are considerably less active in introducing bills alone: The expected number of single-authored bills decreases by factor 0.4, holding all other variables constant. Having had to compete against two challengers in the second round of the elections, increases the average number of single-authored bills by 89 percent, holding everything else equal. A judicial background more than doubles the expected number of bills, holding the other variables constant. For a standard deviation increase in the electoral margin, the mean bill sponsorship productivity increases by 36 percent, holding everything else equal. A standard deviation increase in age (approximately nine years) relates to a 34 percent decrease in the expected number of bills, holding all other factors constant.

The following factors create a scenario in which the theoretical model predicts the highest level of activity: an opposition MP belongs to a non-cohesive party, had to compete against a second challenger in the second round of the elections, comes from a constituency with a high level of local newspaper readers and which does not belong to the hexagon (the European mainland), has a judicial background and past legislative experience, and is average (mean or mode values) on all mixed indicators and control variables. For such a case the empirical model predicts the MP to sponsor 14 bills. The other extreme is a gov-

[128] For the total number of bills the results imply that opposition MPs introduce factor 2.9 more bills than government MPs.

ernment MP from a cohesive party from the Île-de-France, with neither judicial background, nor past legislative experience and again average on the rest of the variables. This case results in the prediction of no single-authored bill being sponsored (or to be exact: 0.09 bills being sponsored on average).

Regression model 3 explains the number of *multi-authored bills* submitted by an MP with the support of at least one other MP but without the support of the entire party group. All effects have the same sign as in model 2, but only the variables discussed in the following reach the standard levels of statistical significance: As in all models, the indicators for party sanctioning potential reach the highest level of statistical significance. In addition to these two factors, the variables "judicial experience", "special post", "constituency size", and "early end" are statistically significant. Having a judicial background, occupying a special post, being from a larger constituency, or leaving parliament early increases the number of cooperative bills without group support.

In the last column of Table 23 the number of *group-supported bills* sponsored by an MP constitute the dependent variable. As expected, these group-sponsored bills follow a different mechanism than do single-authored or multi-authored bills that did not find the support of the entire group. Opposition MPs sponsor such bills less frequently (-55 percent) whereas the expected number of group-supported bills per MP rises by 133 percent for members of cohesive party groups, holding all other variables constant. None of the indicators for constituency sanctioning potential reaches conventional levels of statistical significance. Concerning the individual costs, judicial experience is irrelevant, but previous experience as a member of parliament increases the expected number of group bills. The indicator for the distance between the positions of the parliamentary party group and the constituency is not statistically significant, but switches signs, which indicates that MPs whose constituents have diverging interests are rather less likely to sponsor such bills. Of the mixed indicators, holding a higher office in parliament or in the party as well as having won the election with a higher margin increase the expected number of group bills at statistically significant levels. Neither the constituency size nor an early end of the mandate have a systematic effect on the number of group-supported bills. The number of cases is lower in model 4 than in the other models (545 instead of 551 MPs) because the MPs who never belonged to any party group and consequently never had the chance to sponsor a group-supported bill, were left out of the regression.

Figure 13 shows the difference in predicted probabilities for the number of bills introduced by "extreme types" of MPs as described above. As one can easily see the patterns for single-authored bills and co-authored (non-group supported) bills resemble one another.

Figure 13 Difference in Predicted Probabilities for Bill Sponsorship of Extreme Types of MPs

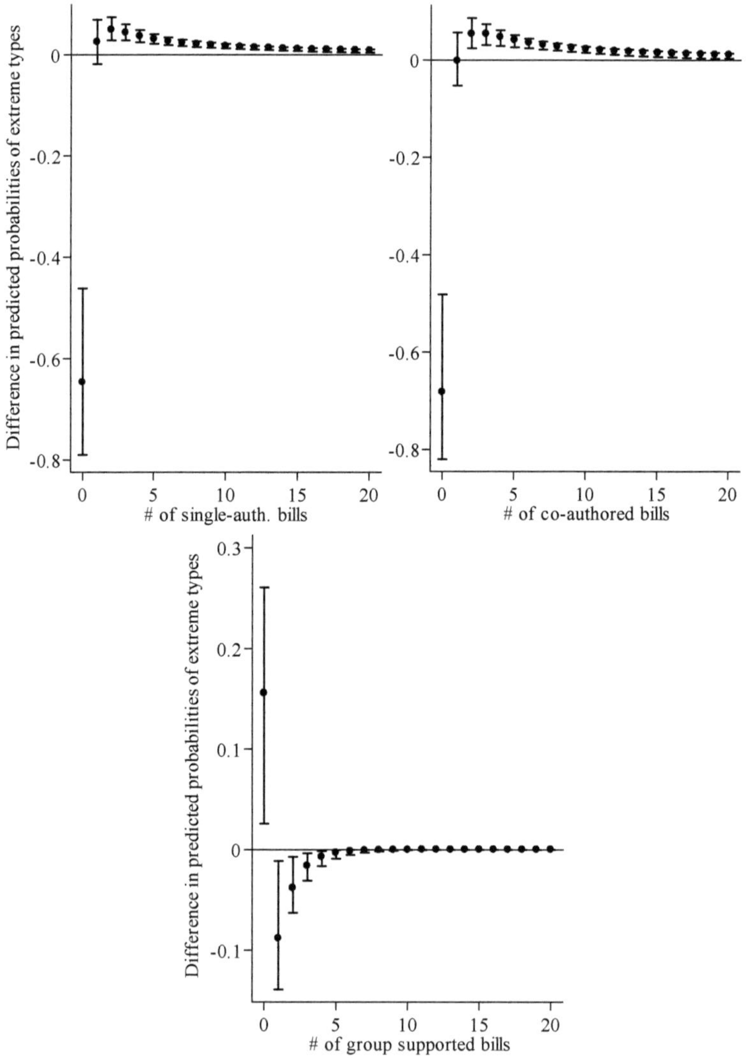

Note: The standard errors of the differences in predicted probabilities (high minus low activity type) were derived using simulation techniques as described in Brambor et al. (2006). The whiskers represent 95 percent confidence intervals.

An MP with characteristics that predict high legislative activities (opposition, non-cohesive party group, second challenger in second round of elections, strong local press, not from the European mainland, judicial background, and past legislative experience) has a considerably lower probability of introducing no bill at all than an MP with opposite characteristics (government party, cohesive party group, Île-de-France, neither judicial background, nor past legislative experience). The probability for introducing more than one bill is significantly higher for the first mentioned type as theoretically predicted. For group supported bills one can observe the reverse relationship: The characteristics associated with more single- and co-authored bills lead to a significantly higher probability of introducing zero group supported bills. And they are also associated with a significantly lower probability of introducing one or more of these bills.

4.3.6 Discussion

Overall, the results in Table 23 lend support to the theoretical model developed in section 4.2. Especially the motivations to sponsor single-authored bills are covered quite well by the model. Here the empirical implications derived from the theoretical model were mostly supported by the empirical test. The strongest support could be found for a high party sanctioning potential decreasing the overall number of bills introduced (Hypothesis 1).

At least partial evidence for a higher number of bills given a higher constituency sanctioning potential was detected (Hypothesis 2).

Also the hypothesized relationship between lower individual costs for drafting a bill and an increased bill sponsorship activity was confirmed (Hypothesis 3). For the mixed indicators holding a special post increased the number of bill sponsored significantly in all regressions with the exception of single-authored bills. The presumed higher independence does not lead to significantly more single-authored bills in order to signal deviation from the official party line. This is probably due to the fact that high party officials are seen as representatives of the party line anyway. Their powerful position enables them to influence the party position directly instead of having to signal deviation. For the age of an MP and the marginality of his district no clear predictions were made. Empirically it could be shown that younger MPs are more active in sponsoring bills on their own. Building an individual profile seems to be more important than fearing career obstacles within the party by showing too much independence. The results for marginality of a district suggest that the effect of winning by a large margin leading to independence of the parliamentary party group is stronger than the effect of reducing the constituency's sanctioning potential. Sending an individual signal still seems important also for MPs who already have quite a save position. While MPs who only won by a few votes seem to rather use other means than bill introduction in order to signal deviation or alternatively they try to appeal to the voters on other aspects which the voters consider in their voting decision.

Only the measure for positional differences (Hypothesis 4) failed to provide any statistically significant support. Actual positional data for party groups and an MP's constituency should be used in future research. Also the indicator for the attention the constituency pays to the activities of their MP at the national level (Île-de-France) did not provide the expected results. Again, future research should try to find better data to measure this aspect of the constituency's sanctioning potential to provide further evidence whether the theoretical predictions are wrong or whether there better data reveals the expected effects.

The results for the co-authored non-group bills show that the effects have a similar direction; however, overall only four independent variables show statistically significant effects. One part of the explanation for the insignificance of many indicators of the theoretical concepts might be that there are several diverse mechanisms motivating the introduction of co-authored bills. A considerable number might be the result of the mechanisms theorized about above, where MPs want to distinguish themselves from the official party line, and cooperation is the result of similar interests. However, the mechanisms might differ if the co-authored bills reflect the position of a party faction. If these bills are not directed primarily at the constituency but rather at the other MPs in the party group, the driving force might less be constituency factors, but internal party organization and an MP's position within the party network. This might explain the positive effect of having a special office within a party or parliament. Another explanation could apply for the insignificant results of the individual cost factors: While having no past legislative experience or judicial background might discourage an MP to introduce a bill on his own, it might even encourage the MP to look for someone with more experience and expertise for cooperation.[129] The finding that MPs from larger constituencies are more active sponsoring co-authored bills than their colleagues from smaller constituencies could mean that larger constituencies are faced with similar problems (instead of more particular problems of smaller constituencies) which makes MPs from these constituencies more likely to introduce bills together with others. It might also mean that representing a large constituency makes it easier to find other MPs who support one's cause. Yet another effect might be that voters in smaller constituencies are more easily reached by other means than putting an issue on the national agenda. Therefore

[129] The question whether inexperienced MPs without the necessary expertise cooperate with more experienced MPs with supplementary expertise or whether rather MPs with similar experience and similar interest work together, could be answered using network analysis.

MPs from smaller constituencies might invest their resources differently. The positive effect of leaving parliament early on the number of single- and co-authored bills is difficult to interpret as there are diverse reasons for such an "early end" reaching from annulment of the election, over election to the Senate, or receiving a government position, to death.[130]

The results for the group-supported bills clearly indicate that their introduction follows other mechanisms. A higher sanctioning potential of an MP's party group leads to an increased expected number of group supported bills. This might be due to a logic of sticks and carrots: On the one hand the party group has more power to force its members to work for the party as a whole instead of pursuing particularistic interests, on the other hand it is also more attractive to invest resources to work for a strong party group as it has better means to reward this activity. In addition to rewards from the party group – be it posts, support in the next electoral campaign or the like – there is also the chance for government MPs to actually receive policy rewards when the bill actually succeeds. The party group bills also serve as policy signals of the position a party group takes on an issue. Therefore it is not surprising that the electorally most successful MPs and the ones with special posts within the party or parliament are more active in sponsoring group bills than their colleagues.

4.4 Conclusion

In this chapter, the question whether a member of parliament sponsors a bill was modeled as a decision theoretic question: A utility maximizing MP is on the one hand confronted with costs for introducing a bill and on the other hand with a party group and constituency voters who have different positions and who sanction (with different strength) the deviation from their respective positions. From this attempt to formalize the decision of an MP, hypotheses were derived and tested empirically using count models. Although the empirical tests partly suffer from crude measurements of the key concepts the results suggest that the theoretical model explains at least a specific part of the bill sponsorship behavior of individual MPs. Particularly bills that are introduced by MPs individually, that is, without the support of others, seem to follow the mechanisms described above. The evidence for co-authored bills without group support is less strong. Here analyzing the co-sponsorship networks could help to distinguish between bills that signal deviation from the party line due to constituency pressure and

130 A more refined measure controlling for the diverse causes of "early end" could not be constructed due to the small number of cases for each category.

bills that signal the position of party factions originating from other factors than constituency. Bills that are supported by the entire party group obviously follow different mechanisms.

Overall it could be shown that bills originating from parliament serve different functions: They can be used by individual MPs to signal deviation from the party line and concern with their voters' positions to their constituency. But bills also serve the function of signaling the policy position of party groups or subgroups. The findings of this chapter show that it is important to distinguish between different functions of bills and also to consider incentives of individual MPs when studying bill introduction in parliamentary democracies, at least in the cases where bill sponsorship is an individual activity.

4.5 Appendix to Chapter 4

Table 24 Summary Statistics of the Independent Variables (for 551 MPs)

Variable	Mean	Std. Dev.	Min	Max
Opposition	0.452	0.498	0	1
Cohesion	0.726	0.446	0	1
Third Party	0.138	0.345	0	1
Île-de-France	0.172	0.378	0	1
Judicial Experience	0.098	0.298	0	1
Several LPs	0.677	0.468	0	1
Overseas Const.	0.027	0.163	0	1
Age	52.814	8.966	31.238	85.710
Accumulation	1.365	1.082	0	4
Electoral Margin	0.148	0.169	0	1
Special Post	0.158	0.365	0	1
Constituency Size*	10.576	1.915	3.440	18.813
Early End	0.109	0.312	0	1
Days in Parliament (as Exposure Time)	1749.142	315.733	145	1850

* Constituency size in 10,000 inhabitants.

Table 25 Number of Bills per MP (for the Regression Sample)

# of Bills Sponsored	# of MPs (Total Bills)	# of MPs (Single-authored)	# of MPs (Co-authored – non-group)	# of MPs (Group supported)
0	251	399	359	432
1	83	71	71	59
2	56	24	35	18

3	38	11	29	13
4	27	19	17	8
5	17	5	12	4
6	17	6	9	5
7	12	5	5	1
8	12	1	3	1
9	3	1	1	1
10	4	1	1	0
11	5	1	1	1
12	3	2	2	0
13	2	0	2	0
14	1	0	1	0
15	3	1	1	1
16	2	1	0	0
17	3	0	1	0
18	4	1	1	0
19	2	0	0	1
22	2	1	0	0
23	1	0	0	0
24	1	0	0	0
25	0	1	0	0
26	1	0	0	0
44	1	0	0	0
Total	551	551	551	545

5 Conclusion

At the beginning of this study on parliamentary bill introduction stood the puzzle of why members of the opposition and backbenchers introduce bills, when the chances of adoption are almost nil: Government control of the legislative agenda makes direct policy influence through oppositional and backbench initiatives a hopeless endeavor. Are these bills then merely "much ado about nothing"? Or do they serve another objective than directly influencing policy?

In this study, I have argued that the introduction of bills by the opposition and by backbenchers is not about direct policy influence. Instead, the dominant incentives for such bills are *vote-seeking* in nature.[131] For the opposition, bill introduction can be seen as a more elaborate tool of opposition than oral and written questions, interpellations, press releases, parliamentary debate, and other instruments. Bills can in fact be used to signal own policy positions and to show alternatives to government policies. Or they can point at topics that rank high on the public agenda but low on the government agenda. For individual opposition MPs and government backbenchers, they can also be a means to build up an independent personal profile.

The example of the coffee tax discussion in 1950s Germany, in the introductory chapter of this study, showed these motivations and gave some insights in the strategic interaction of political actors. For another telling example, which likewise illustrates the findings of Chapter 2 and Chapter 3, Germany's recent decision to phase out nuclear energy suggests itself. While there are good reasons to think that bills and other parliamentary activities are reflections of party positions and priorities (as assumed in Chapter 2), this is certainly not the whole story, as the 2011 nuclear phaseout once again demonstrates.

In the year 2000, the SPD-Green coalition under Chancellor Schröder and Germany's major energy providers had reached an "atomic consensus", which had been in line with the coalition partners' electoral promises. In 2001, a government bill (printed paper of the Bundesrat DRS 705/01) implementing the "atomic consensus" was introduced in Bundesrat and Bundestag and adopted in 2002. The oppositional CDU and FDP signaled their concerns about the phasing-

[131] This does of course not exclude that seeking votes is a means to increase the chances of winning office and then changing policy.

out of nuclear power with a number of parliamentary activities, such as motions as well as minor and major interpellations.

After Schröder lost the elections in 2005, Chancellor Merkel and her Christian Democrats entered government. They were more supportive of nuclear energy, but during the "grand coalition" of CDU and SPD from 2005 through 2009 nuclear energy policies were not changed, as the Social Democrats stood to their electoral promise. Legislative activities on the issue were rare at the time. The Green party introduced some motions that demanded the immediate shutdown of the oldest nuclear power plants, whereas the FDP in turn entered motions to "take climate change seriously" and therefore extend the life of nuclear power plants.

After the 2009 elections Chancellor Merkel was able to form a coalition with the nuclear energy-friendly FDP, and within a year they changed the law and significantly extended the duration during which nuclear power plants could still be operated. The Greens and the SPD reacted with motions, interpellations, and questions to signal their opposition to the government's decision. Up to this point, the reactions of all actors were clearly in line with their election manifestos.[132]

In the wake of the nuclear catastrophe in Fukushima, Japan, in March 2011, "nothing was as before" – a phrase many politicians who had previously supported the use of nuclear energy would use to justify a radical positional turn. In how far their beliefs about the risks of nuclear power plants had indeed changed is difficult to assess. Without a doubt, public awareness of the problem had changed: The "Politbarometer"-survey at the beginning of April 2011 reported that only nine percent of the respondents were in favor of CDU/FDP plans to rely upon nuclear power until 2035. 34 percent stated that they preferred the version of the law passed by the SPD/Green coalition under Schröder, which would put an end to the use of nuclear energy in Germany in 2021. 55 percent demanded to get out of nuclear power as fast as possible.[133] Even among CDU supporters more than 53 percent agreed in mid-April that Germany should shut down nuclear power plants earlier, irrespective of what other European states would do.[134] In addition to positional shifts also the salience of the issue on the public agenda had dramatically increased.

132 The policy stability manifested by the inaction of government on this issue during the "Grand Coalitions" when the winset of the status quo was empty, is a nice example of Tsebelis' veto player theory (Tsebelis 2002).

133 http://www.forschungsgruppe.de/Umfragen/Politbarometer/Archiv/Politbarometer_2011/April_I/, accessed on 23 November 2011.

134 http://www.forschungsgruppe.de/Umfragen/Politbarometer/Archiv/Politbarometer_2011/April_II/, accessed on 23 November 2011.

Only four days after the earthquake and tsunami in Japan, the Green party reacted and introduced a bill (printed paper of the Bundestag DRS 17/5035) to restore the "nuclear compromise" of the SPD/Green government. Eleven days after the events another bill (DRS 17/5180) followed asking for the eight most dangerous nuclear power plants to be closed down without any compensation. And in May 2011 (DRS 17/5180), a bill to shut down the last nuclear plant in 2017 (DRS 17/5931) was introduced. The SPD also reacted with a legislative initiative (DRS 17/5179) within eleven days after Fukushima. The bill made the same claims as the two Green bills, namely to reestablish the old "nuclear compromise" and to shut down the eight oldest nuclear power plants in Germany. The PDS, which had not been active on the issue before, took the longest of the three opposition parties to respond to the new situation. One month after the nuclear catastrophe in Japan, the PDS sponsored two bills, one proposing that the ban of nuclear energy should be written in the constitution, the other one asking to prohibit the transfer of energy production rights from the closed down older nuclear power plants to newer ones.

The government and the majority parties in parliament reacted even slower in the legislative arena. It took them until the beginning of June to introduce two identical bills, which the government introduced to the Bundesrat (DRS 340/11) and which the party groups of CDU/CSU and FDP introduced in the Bundestag (DRS 17/6070). The bills were joined in the process, passed the Bundestag within a month and became effective two months after the introduction. The core of the new legislation was the nuclear phaseout until the end of the year 2022. At the end of June, the Green party came up with another legislative initiative (DRS 17/6203), which demanded, as did the PDS, to include an article banning nuclear power in the constitution.

The (more or less) immediate reactions of political actors from across the political spectrum to public opinion were certainly exceptional. They were spurred by the clarity of the public signal, as well as by the parliamentary elections in three German Länder at the end of March, which were interpreted as a "referendum on nuclear energy" by some politicians (compare, in particular, the landslide victory of the Green party in Baden-Württemberg in March 2011, which put an end to almost 60 years of continuous CDU minister-presidents).

The political events and initiatives surrounding Germany's nuclear phaseout in 2011 once again illustrate the results of Chapters 2 and 3, which have shown evidence for the use of bills as programmatic signals as well as for the responsiveness of parliamentary activities to public opinion. Bills and other parliamentary activities are sometimes used as signals of policy positions (see Chapter 2), as when opposition to government proposals was signaled in the pre-Fukushima legislative periods. Or they are reactions to public opinion (see Chapter 3), as when all parties prioritized the issue nuclear phaseout after Fukushima.

In Chapter 2 of this study, a model of oppositional bill introduction as strategic signaling of parties' policy positions was formalized. The analysis of the patterns of bill introduction over different policy dimensions in Belgium, France, Germany, and the United Kingdom found evidence for a central empirical implication of the theoretical model, namely that political actors introduce more bills on a policy dimension on which they have a more central position. In addition, the salience of policy dimensions and the seat share of an actor have the predicted positive effect. However, the results do not provide unambiguous support of the model of bills as policy signals. Differences between the countries can be interpreted as evidence for something other than partisan logic driving at least parts of bill introduction. The aspect that – depending on the possibilities of MPs and the electoral incentives – bills could also serve as a means to pursue a personal vote was taken up in Chapter 4.

Overall, the results of Chapter 2 provided good evidence for the usage of bills as policy signals in order to win votes. However, vote-seeking should not only take place through signaling the position of the party's policy program. In order to gain votes, parties should be especially aware of dealing with issues that are important to voters. This aspect of bill introduction was examined in more detail in Chapter 3. While bills often reflect a party's position and priorities, as stated in party manifestos, the Fukushima example shows that positions as well as priorities can be affected by important events in combination with public opinion. Chapter 3 dealt more generally with the questions whether and how the parliamentary activities of political actors respond to public opinion, whether there are differences between the responses of opposition, government, and parliamentary majority, and in how far upcoming elections influence responsiveness to public opinion. The results confirm a close relationship between public opinion and parliamentary activities. In addition, differences between the different political actors can be observed. Higher levels of public attention lead to more parliamentary activities of the opposition. With restrictions this is also true for the government parties in parliament. However, as expected, the connection between public opinion and parliamentary activities is less direct for government. Evidence for strategic responsiveness in the light of upcoming elections can again be found foremost for opposition parties.

In Chapter 4 the focus shifted to vote-seeking incentives of individual MPs, which might influence bill sponsorship behavior. Bill sponsorship was modeled as a possibility to signal an individual position to the constituency. Drawn between constituency demands and party line, MPs have to decide whether or not to make use of bill introduction. The empirical test suggests that the theoretical model explains at least a specific part of the bill sponsorship behavior of individual MPs. Particularly bills that are introduced by MPs individually closely follow the proclaimed mechanisms. Patterns of introduction of co-authored bills are not explained as well by the model. And as expected, bills supported by the entire party group follow different mechanisms. This points to the fact that parliamentary bills can serve different functions: They can be used by individual MPs to signal their constituency deviation from the party line and concern with their voters' positions. But bills also serve the function of signaling the policy position of party groups or subgroups.

Implications of the Findings and Paths for Future Research

The findings described above have important implications for the analysis of bill introduction. Treating all bills equally diverts from the diverse mechanisms being at work. Disaggregating the data could uncover a more nuanced picture of legislative activity by parties and individual MPs. Bills – and probably also other legislative activities such as written or oral questions, legislative speech etc. – serve as tools in inter-party competition but also as tools for individual reelection. MPs can use these tools jointly with other means to increase the visibility of the party position among the voters as well as their own visibility within the party, or they can build up their individual reputation by targeting their constituency in deviation from the party line.

Further research could attempt a consolidation of the party level model and the individual level model of bill introduction. While in the German institutional context party factors can be expected to dominate, in a political system like Belgium one can expect both factors to be at work. An integrated model could make more fine-grained predictions for different institutional contexts. Empirically, this study has found evidence that patterns of bill introduction are in line with vote-seeking considerations of political actors. An interesting next step would be to analyze the impact of bill sponsorship behavior on the electoral results of parties or individual MPs.

Chapter 3 provides good evidence for responsive behavior of parliamentary opposition in Germany, and also, with some restrictions, for the responsive behavior of government and its parliamentary majority. Further research should extend the range of time and space of this study in order to see whether these findings are generalizable to other contexts. For the German case going back in time is restricted by the lack of "most important problem" data. Future research might be able to use the data that is currently assembled for the comparative agendas project.[135] Such data would also allow for the extension of the number of issues treated. An extension that includes more governments and more issues could answer the question whether the salience actors attach to an issue in their electoral programs matters for responsiveness. Disaggregating the political actors and time would enable refined answers to questions of inter-party dynamics. However, the availability of public opinion data still is a restricting factor here. A comparative perspective would give insight into the role that strong national parties play with regard to responsiveness to general public opinion. In parliamentary systems in which parliamentary activities are in the hands of individual MPs and where personal vote-seeking incentives prevail, MPs might focus on their local constituencies, which might lead to a reduced responsiveness to the national public agenda.

The model of private members' bills introduction developed in Chapter 4 should also be applied to other institutional contexts to test whether the findings can be generalized. MPs in the United Kingdom are expected to have incentives comparable to their French colleagues caused by the electoral system; however, their possibilities of bill introduction are much more limited due to more restrictive rules. The Belgian electoral setup with multimember districts and preferential list PR with preference votes produces a quite different strategic environment for MPs than is the case in France. But even for MPs in Belgium, Bräuninger et al. (2012) find evidence for the usage of legislative proposals as means to improve the chances of reselection and reelection. In Germany, individual signaling through bills is hardly possible, as the right of initiating legislation from within parliament lies in the hands of parliamentary party groups or groups of MPs comprising at least five percent of the parliamentarians. But also in this institutional context MPs can individually contribute to the drafting of bills or sign bills to explicitly state their support. Bräuninger and Brunner (2009) show that among other factors the mode of election and the geographic origin influence co-sponsorship patterns. This can be seen as an indication that even in Germany bill (co-)sponsorship is influenced by electoral considerations and constituency interests.

In sum, this study shows that Olson and Norton's (1996: 7) so-called 90 percent rule ("In most cases, the 90 per cent rule applies, with 90 per cent of legislative activity being initiated by the executive, which gets 90 per cent of what it wants") is not true – in most parliamentary democracies a significant proportion of bills stems from the parliamentary floor, especially from opposition parties. Notwithstanding the low chances of getting these bills adopted, this behavior is not irrational but can be explained systematically. Some proportion

[135] http://www.comparativeagendas.org/germany, accessed on 3 August 2011.

can be accounted for by actual policy-seeking. However, other motivations seem more important: With this study, I have shown systematically that vote-seeking motivations of parties and individual MPs can account for empirically observed patterns of bill introduction. The major innovations of the research constituting this study are the development of consistent formal models for the party and the individual level and the empirical test of the model implications, the shift of focus away from policy output to policy input and to the motivation of opposition, which is often neglected in research, and finally the adoption of an individual level perspective in research on bill sponsorship in parliamentary democracies. The results of this study show that parliamentary initiatives are not simply "much ado about nothing", but that vote-seeking motivations are helpful to explain patterns of oppositional and backbench bill introduction.

6 References

Achen, Christopher H. 2000. "Why Lagged Dependent Variables Can Suppress the Explanatory Power of Other Independent Variables." Paper prepared for the Annual Meeting of the Political Methodology Section of the American Political Science Association, Los Angeles, USA, 20-22 July 2000.

Adams, James, Andrea B. Haupt, and Heather Stoll. 2009. "What Moves Parties? The Role of Public Opinion and Global Economic Conditions in Western Europe." *Comparative Political Studies* 42 (5): 611-39.

Aldrich, John H., James E. Alt, and Arthur Lupia. 2008. "The EITM Approach: Origins and Interpretations." In *The Oxford Handbook of Political Methodology*, ed. Janet M. Box-Steffensmeier, Henry E. Brady, and David Collier. Oxford: Oxford University Press, 828-43.

Alesina, Alberto, John Londregan, and Howard Rosenthal. 1993. "A Model of the Political Economy of the United States." *American Political Science Review* 87 (1): 12-33.

Alesina, Alberto, and Howard Rosenthal. 1995. *Partisan Politics, Divided Government, and the Economy.* Cambridge: Cambridge University Press.

Andersen, Robert, James Tilley, and Anthony F. Heath. 2005. "Political Knowledge and Enlightened Preferences: Party Choice through the Electoral Cycle." *British Journal of Political Science* 35 (2): 285-302.

Andeweg, Rudy B., and Lia Nijzink. 1995. "Beyond the Two-Body Image: Relations between Ministers and MPs." In *Parliaments and Majority Rule in Western Europe*, ed. Herbert Döring. Frankfurt am Main: Campus, 152-78.

Ansolabehere, Stephen, James M. Snyder Jr., and Charles Stewart III. 2001. "Candidate Positioning in U.S. House Elections." *American Journal of Political Science* 45 (1): 136-59.

Arter, David. 2006. "Conclusion. Questioning the 'Mezey Question': An Interrogatory Framework for the Comparative Study of Legislatures." *Journal of Legislative Studies* 12 (3-4): 462-82.

Auffermann, Burkhard, and Seppo Laakso. 2008. "Gesetzgebung im politischen System Finnlands." In *Gesetzgebung in Westeuropa*, ed. Wolfgang Ismayr. Wiesbaden: VS Verlag für Sozialwissenschaften, 65-97.

Aurelio, Tobias, and Michael J. Campbell. 1998. "Time Series Regression for Counts Allowing for Autocorrelation." *Stata Technical Bulletin* 46: 33-37.

Austen-Smith, David, and Jeffrey Banks. 1988. "Elections, Coalitions, and Legislative Outcomes." *American Political Science Review* 82 (2): 405-22.

Axelrod, Robert. 1970. *Conflict of Interest.* Chicago: Markham.

Barnello, Michelle A., and Kathleen A. Bratton. 2007. "Bridging the Gender Gap in Bill Sponsorship." *Legislative Studies Quarterly* 32 (3): 449-74.

Baron, David P., and John A. Ferejohn. 1989. "Bargaining in Legislatures." *American Political Science Review* 83 (4): 1181-206.

Bartels, Larry M. 1991. "Constituency Opinion and Congressional Policy Making: The Reagan Defense Build Up." *American Political Science Review* 85 (2): 457-74.

Baumgartner, Frank R., Christian Breunig, Christoffer Green-Pedersen, Bryan D. Jones, Peter B. Mortensen, Michiel Nuytemans, and Stefaan Walgrave. 2009. "Punctuated Equilibrium in Comparative Perspective." *American Journal of Political Science* 53: 603-20.

Baumgartner, Frank R., and Bryan D. Jones. 1993. *Agendas and Instability in American Politics.* Chicago: University of Chicago Press.

Baumgartner, Frank R., Bryan D. Jones, and John Wilkerson. 2011. "Comparative Studies of Policy Dynamics." *Comparative Political Studies* 44 (8): 947-72.

Becher, Michael, and Ulrich Sieberer. 2008. "Discipline, Electoral Rules and Defection in the Bundestag, 1983-94." *German Politics* 17 (3): 293-304.

Becker, Rolf, and Thomas Saalfeld. 2004. "The Life and Times of Bills." In *Patterns of Parliamentary Behavior: Passage of Legislation across Western Europe*, ed. Herbert Döring and Mark Hallerberg. Aldershot: Ashgate, 57-90.

Behnke, Joachim. 2005. "Lassen sich Signifikanztests auf Vollerhebungen anwenden? Einige essayistische Anmerkungen." *Politische Vierteljahresschrift* 46 (1): O1-O15.

Benoit, Kenneth, Thomas Bräuninger, and Marc Debus. 2009. "Challenges for Estimating Policy Preferences: Announcing an Open Access Archive of Political Documents." *German Politics* 18 (3): 441-54.

Benoit, Kenneth, and Michael Laver. 2003. "Estimating Irish Party Policy Positions using Computer Wordscoring: The 2002 Election." *Irish Political Studies* 18 (1): 97-107.

Benoit, Kenneth, and Michael Laver. 2006. *Party Policy in Modern Democracies.* London: Routledge.

Berk, Richard A., Bruce Western, and Robert E. Weiss. 1995a. "Statistical Inference for Apparent Populations." *Sociological Methodology* 25: 421-58.

Berk, Richard A., Bruce Western, and Robert E. Weiss. 1995b. "Reply to Bollen, Firebaugh, and Rubin." *Sociological Methodology* 25: 481-85.

Bernauer, Julian, and Thomas Bräuninger. 2009. "Intra-Party Preference Heterogeneity and Faction Membership in the 15th German Bundestag: A Computational Text Analysis of Parliamentary Speeches." *German Politics* 18 (3): 385-402.

Blais, André. 2006. "The Causes and Consequences of the Cumul des Mandats." *French Politics* 4 (3): 266-68.

Blais, André, and Marc A. Bodet. 2006. "Does Proportional Representation Foster Closer Congruence between Citizens and Policy Makers?" *Comparative Political Studies* 39 (10): 1243-62.

Bollen, Kenneth A. 1995. "Apparent and Nonapparent Significance Tests." *Sociological Methodology* 25: 459-68.

Bowler, Shaun. 2010. "Private Members' Bills in the UK Parliament: Is There an 'Electoral Connection'?" *Journal of Legislative Studies* 16 (4): 476-94.

Brambor, Thomas, William Roberts Clark, and Matt Golder. 2006. "Understanding Interaction Models: Improving Empirical Analyses." *Political Analysis* 14 (1): 63-82.

Brandt, Patrick T., and Todd Sandler. 2012. "A Bayesian Poisson Vector Autoregression Model." *Political Analysis* 20 (3): 292-315.

Brandt, Patrick T., and John T. Williams. 2001. "A Linear Poisson Autoregressive Model: The Poisson AR(p) Model." *Political Analysis* 9 (2): 164-84.

Brandt, Patrick T., John T. Williams, Benjamin O. Fordham, and Brain Pollins. 2000. "Dynamic Modeling for Persistent Event-Count Time Series." *American Journal of Political Science* 44 (4): 823-43.

Bräuninger, Thomas. 2005. "A Partisan Model of Government Expenditure." *Public Choice* 125 (3): 409-29.

Bräuninger, Thomas, and Martin Brunner. 2009. "Cosponsorship Networks in the German Bundestag: Evidence for Personal or Party Behavior?" Paper presented at the 67th Annual National Conference of the Midwest Political Science Association, Chicago, USA, 2-5 April 2009.

Bräuninger, Thomas, Martin Brunner, and Thomas Däubler. 2012. "Individualistic or Party-Oriented Legislative Activity: How Electoral Incentives Shape Belgian MPs' Bill Initiation Strategies." *European Journal of Political Research* 51 (5): 607-45.

Bräuninger, Thomas, and Marc Debus. 2010. "The Sources of Bipartisan Politics in Parliamentary Democracies." In *Reform Processes and Policy Change: Veto Players and Decision-Making in Modern Democracies*, ed. Thomas König, George Tsebelis, and Marc Debus. New York: Springer, 145-64.

Bräuninger, Thomas, and Marc Debus. 2012. *Parteienwettbewerb in den deutschen Bundesländern.* Wiesbaden: VS Verlag für Sozialwissenschaften.

Bräuninger, Thomas, Marc Debus, and Fabian Wüst. 2008. "Governments, Parliaments, and Legislative Activity." Unpublished manuscript.

Bräuninger, Thomas, Thomas Gschwend, and Susumu Shikano. 2010. "Sachpolitik oder Parteipolitik? Eine Bestimmung des Parteidrucks im Bundesrat mittels bayesianischer Methoden." *Politische Vierteljahresschrift* 51 (2): 223-49.

Bräuninger, Thomas, and Thomas König. 1999. "The Checks and Balances of Party Federalism: German Federal Government in a Divided Legislature." *European Journal of Political Research* 36 (2): 207-34.

Bräuninger, Thomas, and Thomas König. 2000. "Regieren im Föderalismus." Final Report to the Federal Ministry for Education and Research. Unpublished manuscript.

Breeman, Gerard, David Lowery, Caelesta Poppelaars, Sandra L. Resodihardjo, Arco Timmermans, and Jouke De Vries. 2009. "Political Attention in a Coalition System: Analysing Queen's Speeches in the Netherlands 1945-2007." *Acta Politica* 44 (1): 1-27.

Brettschneider, Frank. 1995. *Öffentliche Meinung und Politik: Eine empirische Studie zur Responsivität des deutschen Bundestages zwischen 1949 und 1990.* Opladen: Westdeutscher Verlag.

Bromwich, David. 2000. *On Empire, Liberty, and Reform: Speeches and Letters.* New Haven: Yale University Press.

Broscheid, Andreas, and Thomas Gschwend. 2005. "Zur statistischen Analyse von Vollerhebungen." *Politische Vierteljahresschrift* 46 (1): O16-O26.
Brunner, Martin, and Marc Debus. 2006. "Datensatzerstellung, Codierungsrichtlinien und Codebuch zum Datensatz 'Vergleichende Gesetzgebung'." Unpublished manuscript.
Brunner, Martin, and Marc Debus. 2008. "Between Programmatic Interests and Party Politics: The German Bundesrat in the Legislative Process." *German Politics* 17 (3): 232-51.
Butor, Michel. 1974. "Travel and Writing." *Mosaic* 8 (1): 1-16.
Cain, Bruce, John Ferejohn, and Morris Fiorina. 1987. *The Personal Vote: Constituency Service and Electoral Independence.* Cambridge: Harvard University Press.
Cameron, Adrian Colin, and Pravin K. Trivedi. 1998. *Regression Analysis of Count Data.* 1998. Cambridge: Cambridge University Press.
Cameron, Adrian Colin, and Pravin K. Trivedi. 2001. "Essentials of Count Data Regression." In *A Companion to Theoretical Econometrics*, ed. Badi H. Baltagi. Malden: Blackwell, 331-48.
Campbell, James E. 1982. "Cosponsoring Legislation in the U.S. Congress." *Legislative Studies Quarterly* 7 (3): 415-22.
Carey, John M. 2007. "Competing Principals, Political Institutions, and Party Unity in Legislative Voting." *American Journal of Political Science* 51 (1): 92-107.
Carey, John M., and Matthew Soberg Shugart. 1995. "Incentives to Cultivate a Personal Vote: A Rank Ordering of Electoral Formulas." *Electoral Studies* 14 (4): 417-39.
Childs, Sarah, and June Withey. 2004. "Women Representatives Acting for Women: Sex and the Signing of Early Day Motions in the 1997 British Parliament." *Political Studies* 52 (3): 552-64.
Clark, Janet. 1998. "Women at the National Level: An Update on Roll-Call Voting Behavior." In *Women and Elective Office: Past, Present, and Future*, ed. Sue Thomas and Clyde Wilcox. Oxford: Oxford University Press, 118-29.
Claro da Fonseca, Sara, and Ana Maria Guerra Martins. 2008. "Gesetzgebung im politischen System Portugals." In *Gesetzgebung in Westeuropa*, ed. Wolfgang Ismayr. Wiesbaden: VS Verlag für Sozialwissenschaften, 559-613.
Collie, Melissa P. 1984. "Voting Behavior in Legislatures." *Legislative Studies Quarterly* 9 (1): 3-50.
Cook, Timothy E. 1989. *Making Laws and Making News: Media Strategies in the U.S. House of Representatives.* Washington: Brookings Institution Press.
Cox, Gary W. 2006. "The Organization of Democratic Legislatures." In *The Oxford Handbook of Political Economy*, ed. Barry R. Weingast and Donald A. Wittmann. Oxford: Oxford University Press, 141-61.
Crespin, Michael H. 2010. "Serving Two Masters: Redistricting and Voting in the U.S. House of Representatives." *Political Research Quarterly* 63 (4): 850-59.
Cusack, Thomas R. 2001. "Partisanship in the Setting and Coordination of Fiscal and Monetary Policies." *European Journal of Political Research* 40 (1): 93-115.
Däubler, Thomas. 2011. "Bills from the Floor: Why Governing Party Groups Initiate Their Own Legislation." *Journal of Legislative Studies* 17 (4): 435-57.

Debus, Marc. 2008. "Unfulfilled Promises? German Social Democrats and their Policy Positions at the Federal and State Level between 1994 and 2006." *Journal of Elections, Public Opinion & Parties* 18 (2): 201-24.

Depré, Sébastien, and David Renders. 1996. "Le partage des compétences législatives entre les assemblées fédérales." *Annales de droit de Louvain* 56 (3): 331-56.

De Winter, Lieven, and Patrick Dumont. 2003. "Delegation and Accountability Under Partitocratic Rule." In *Delegation and Accountability in Parliamentary Democracies*, ed. Kaare Strøm, Wolfgang C. Müller, and Torbjörn Bergman. Oxford: Oxford University Press, 253-80.

De Winter, Lieven, and Patrick Dumont. 2006. "Do Belgian Parties Undermine the Democratic Chain of Delegation?" *West European Politics* 29 (5): 957-76.

Döring, Herbert. 1995a. "Fewer Though Presumably More Conflictual Bills: Parliamentary Government Acting as a Monopolist." In *Parliaments and Majority Rule in Western Europe*, ed. Herbert Döring. Frankfurt am Main: Campus, 593-600.

Döring, Herbert. 1995b. "Is Government Control of the Agenda Likely to Keep 'Legislative Inflation' at Bay?" In *Parliaments and Majority Rule in Western Europe*, ed. Herbert Döring. Frankfurt am Main: Campus, 654-87.

Döring, Herbert, ed. 1995c. *Parliaments and Majority Rule in Western Europe*. Frankfurt am Main: Campus.

Downs, Anthony. 1957. *An Economic Theory of Democracy*. New York: Harper & Row.

Duhamel, Olivier, and Jean-Luc Parodi. 1988. *La Constitution de la Cinquième République*. Paris: Presses de la Fondation Nationale des Sciences Politiques.

Easton, David. 1953. *The Political System: An Inquiry into the State of Political Science*. New York: Knopf.

Erikson, Robert S. 1978. "Constituency Opinion and Congressional Behavior: A Reexamination of the Miller-Stokes Representation Data." *American Journal of Political Science* 22 (3): 511-35.

Eulau, Heinz, and Paul D. Karps. 1977. "The Puzzle of Representation: Specifying Components of Responsiveness." *Legislative Studies Quarterly* 2 (3): 233-54.

Fiorina, Morris P. 1973. "Electoral Margins, Constituency Influence, and Policy Moderation: A Critical Assessment." *American Politics Research* 1 (4): 479-98.

Fiorina, Morris P. 1974. *Representatives, Roll Calls, and Constituencies*. Lexington: Lexington Books.

Firebaugh, Glenn. 1995. "Will Bayesian Inference Help? A Skeptical View." *Sociological Methodology* 25: 469-72.

Flinn, Thomas A. 1964. "Party Responsibility in the States: Some Causal Factors." *American Political Science Review* 58 (1): 60-71.

Franklin, Mark N., and Michael Tappin. 1977. "Early Day Motions as Unobtrusive Measures of Backbench Opinion in Britain." *British Journal of Political Science* 7 (1): 49-69.

Freeman, John R. 1983. "Granger Causality and the Times Series Analysis of Political Relationships." *American Journal of Political Science* 27 (2): 327-58.

Freeman, John R., John T. Williams, and Tse-min Lin. 1989. "Vector Autoregression and the Study of Politics." *American Journal of Political Science* 33 (4): 842-77.

Froman, Lewis A. 1963. *Congressmen and Their Constituencies.* Chicago: Rand McNally.

Ganghof, Steffen, and Thomas Bräuninger. 2006. "Government Status and Legislative Behaviour: Partisan Veto Players in Australia, Denmark, Finland and Germany." *Party Politics* 12 (4): 521-39.

Garand, James C., and Kelly M. Burke. 2006. "Legislative Activity and the 1994 Republican Takeover: Exploring Changing Patterns of Sponsorship and Cosponsorship in the U.S. House." *American Politics Research* 34 (2): 159-88.

Gianetti, Daniela, and Michael Laver. 2005. "Policy Positions and Jobs in the Government." *European Journal of Political Research* 44 (1): 91-120.

Gould, Stephen J., and Niles Eldredge. 1993. "Punctuated Equilibrium Comes of Age." *Nature* 366 (6452): 223-7.

Granger, Clive W. J. 1969. "Investigating Causal Relations by Econometric Models and Cross-Spectral Methods." *Econometrica* 37 (3): 424-38.

Green-Pedersen, Christoffer, and Peter B. Mortensen. 2010. "Who Sets the Agenda and Who Responds to It in the Danish Parliament? A New Model of Issue Competition and Agenda-Setting." *European Journal of Political Research* 49 (2): 257-81.

Grofman, Bernard. 2004. "Downs and Two-Party Convergence." *Annual Review of Political Science* 7: 25-46.

Gross, Donald A., and Lee Sigelman. 1984. "Comparing Party Systems: A Multidimensional Approach." *Comparative Politics* 16 (4): 463-79.

Hallerberg, Mark. 2004. "Electoral Laws, Government, and Parliament." In *Patterns of Parliamentary Behavior: Passage of Legislation across Western Europe*, ed. Herbert Döring and Mark Hallerberg. Aldershot: Ashgate, 11-33.

Harward, Brian M., and Kenneth W. Moffett. 2010. "The Calculus of Cosponsorship in the U.S. Senate." *Legislative Studies Quarterly* 35 (1): 117-43.

Helms, Ludger. 2004. "Five Ways of Institutionalizing Political Opposition: Lessons from the Advanced Democracies." *Government and Opposition* 39 (1): 22-54.

Herrick, Rebekah, and Michael K. Moore. 1993. "Political Ambition's Effect on Legislative Behavior: Schlesinger's Typology Reconsidered and Revisited." *Journal of Politics* 55 (3): 765-76.

Hibbs, Douglas A. 1977. "Political Parties and Macroeconomic Policy." *American Political Science Review* 71 (4): 1467-87.

Highton, Benjamin, and Michael S. Rocca. 2005. "Beyond the Roll-Call Arena: The Determinants of Position Taking in Congress." *Political Research Quarterly* 58 (2): 303-16.

Hilbe, Joseph M. 2007. *Negative Binomial Regression.* Cambridge: Cambridge University Press.

Hobolt, Sara Binzer, and Robert Klemmensen. 2008. "Government Responsiveness and Political Competition in Comparative Perspective." *Comparative Political Studies* 41 (3): 309-37.

Hofferbert, Richard I., and Hans-Dieter Klingemann. 1990. "The Policy Impact of Party Programmes and Government Declarations in the Federal Republic of Germany." *European Journal of Political Research* 18 (3): 277-304.

House of Commons. 2010a. "Early Day Motions." Factsheet P3 Procedure Series, available at http://www.parliament.uk/documents/commons-information-office/p03.pdf, accessed on 11 June 2011.

House of Commons. 2010b. "Private Members' Bills Procedure." Factsheet L2 Legislation Series, available at http://www.parliament.uk/documents/commons-information-office/l02.pdf, accessed on 11 June 2011.

Huber, John D., and Bingham G. Powell. 1994. "Congruence between Citizens and Policymakers in Two Visions of Liberal Democracy." *World Politics* 46 (3): 291-326.

Hug, Simon. 2010. "Selection Effects in Roll Call Votes." *British Journal of Political Science* 40 (1): 225-35.

Inter-Parliamentary Union. 1986. *Parliaments of the World: A Comparative Reference Compendium.* 2nd ed. Aldershot: Gower House.

Ismayr, Wolfgang, ed. 2008a. *Gesetzgebung in Westeuropa.* Wiesbaden: VS Verlag für Sozialwissenschaften.

Ismayr, Wolfgang. 2008b. "Gesetzgebung im politischen System Deutschlands." In *Gesetzgebung in Westeuropa*, ed. Wolfgang Ismayr. Wiesbaden: VS Verlag für Sozialwissenschaften, 383-429.

Jann, Werner, and Jan Tiessen. 2008. "Gesetzgebung im politischen System Schwedens." In *Gesetzgebung in Westeuropa*, ed. Wolfgang Ismayr. Wiesbaden: VS Verlag für Sozialwissenschaften, 99-131.

Jennings, Will, Shaun Bevan, Arco Timmermans, Gerard Breeman, Sylvain Brouard, Laura Chaqués-Bonafont, Christoffer Green-Pedersen, Peter John, Peter B. Mortensen, and Anna M. Palau. 2011. "Effects of the Core Functions of Government on the Diversity of Executive Agendas." *Comparative Political Studies* 44 (8): 1001-30.

Jones, Bryan D. 1973. "Competitiveness, Role Orientations, and Legislative Responsiveness." *Journal of Politics* 35 (4): 924-47.

Jones, Bryan D., and Frank R. Baumgartner. 2005. *The Politics of Attention: How Government Prioritizes Problems.* Chicago: University of Chicago Press.

Jones, Bryan D., Heather Larsen-Price, and John Wilkerson. 2009. "Representation and American Governing Institutions." *Journal of Politics* 71 (1): 277-90.

Jung, Robert C., Martin Kukuk, and Roman Liesenfeld. 2006. "Time Series of Count Data: Modeling, Estimation and Diagnostics." *Computational Statistics & Data Analysis* 51 (4): 2350-64.

Kam, Christopher. 2009. *Party Discipline and Parliamentary Politics.* Cambridge: Cambridge University Press.

Keele, Luke, and Nathan J. Kelly. 2006. "Dynamic Models for Dynamic Theories: The Ins and Outs of Lagged Dependent Variables." *Political Analysis* 14 (2): 186-205.

Kessler, Daniel, and Keith Krehbiel. 1996. "Dynamics of Cosponsorship." *American Political Science Review* 90 (3): 555-66.

Key, Valdimer O., Jr. 1961. *Public Opinion and American Democracy.* New York: Knopf.

Kimmel, Adolf. 2008. "Gesetzgebung im politischen System Frankreichs." In *Gesetzgebung in Westeuropa*, ed. Wolfgang Ismayr. Wiesbaden: VS Verlag für Sozialwissenschaften, 229-69.

King, Gary, Robert O. Keohane, and Sidney Verba. 1994. *Designing Social Inquiry: Scientific Inference in Qualitative Research.* Princeton: Princeton University Press.

Klingemann, Hans-Dieter, Richard I. Hofferbert, and Ian Budge. 1994. *Parties, Policies, and Democracy.* Boulder: Westview.

Knapp, Andrew, and Vincent Wright. 2001. *The Government and Politics of France.* London: Routledge.

Krehbiel, Keith. 1998. *Pivotal Politics: A Theory of U.S. Lawmaking.* Chicago: Chicago University Press.

Kuck, Harald. 2011. "Kaffeesteuer: Ein Relikt aus dem 18. Jahrhundert." *Focus Online*, 4 January 2011. Available on http://www.focus.de/finanzen/steuern/verbrauchsteuern/kaffeesteuer_aid_27305.html, accessed on 11 November 2011.

Lancester, Thomas D., and W. David Patterson. 1990. "Comparative Pork Barrel Politics: Perceptions from the West German Bundestag." *Comparative Political Studies* 22 (4): 458-77.

Laver, Michael. 2001. "Position and Salience in the Policies of Political Actors." In *Estimating the Policy Positions of Political Actors*, ed. Michael Laver. London: Routledge, 66-75.

Laver, Michael. 2006. "Legislatures and Parliaments in Comparative Context." In *The Oxford Handbook of Political Economy*, ed. Barry R. Weingast and Donald A. Wittman. Oxford: Oxford University Press, 119-40.

Laver, Michael, and Kenneth Benoit. 2002. "Locating TDs in Policy Spaces: The Computational Text Analysis of Dáil Speeches." *Irish Political Studies* 17 (1): 59-73.

Laver, Michael, Kenneth Benoit, and John Garry. 2003. "Extracting Policy Positions from Political Texts Using Words as Data." *American Political Science Review*, 97 (2): 311-31.

Laver, Michael, and W. Ben Hunt. 1992. *Policy and Party Competition.* New York: Routledge.

Laver, Michael, and Norman J. Schofield. 1998. *Multiparty Government: The Politics of Coalition in Europe.* Ann Arbor: University of Michigan Press.

Laver, Michael, and Kenneth A. Shepsle. 1996. *Making and Breaking Governments. Cabinets and Legislatures in Parliamentary Democracies.* Cambridge: Cambridge University Press.

Leece, John, and Hugh Berrington. 1977. "Measurements of Backbench Attitudes by Guttman Scaling of Early Day Motions: A Pilot Study, Labour, 1968-69." *British Journal of Political Science* 7 (4): 529-49.

Lewis-Beck, Michael S., and Mary Stegmaier. 2000. "Economic Determinants of Electoral Outcomes." *Annual Review of Political Science* 3 (1): 183-219.

Lijphart, Arend. 1999. *Patterns of Democracy: Government Forms and Performance in Thirty-Six Countries.* New Haven: Yale University Press.

Lindon, Denis, and Pierre Weill. 1974. *Le choix d'un député.* Paris: Édition de Minuit.

Long, Scott J., and Jeremy Freese. 2006. *Regression Models for Categorical Dependent Variables Using Stata.* 2nd ed. College Station: Stata Press.

Lupia, Arthur, and Kaare Strøm. 1995. "Coalition Termination and the Strategic Timing of Parliamentary Elections." *American Political Science Review* 89 (3): 648-65.

MacRae, Duncan. 1952. "The Relation between Roll Call Votes and Constituencies in the Massachusetts House of Representatives." *American Political Science Review* 46 (4): 1046-55.

Maltzman, Forrest, and Lee Sigelman. 1996. "The Politics of Talk: Unconstrained Floor Time in the U.S. House of Representatives." *Journal of Politics* 58 (3): 819-30.

Manow, Philip, and Simone Burkhart. 2007. "Legislative Self-Restraint Under Divided Government in Germany, 1976-2002." *Legislative Studies Quarterly* 32 (2): 167-91.

Martin, Lanny W. 2004. "The Government Agenda in Parliamentary Democracies." *American Journal of Political Science* 48 (3): 445-61.

Martin, Lanny W., and Georg Vanberg. 2004. "Policing the Bargain: Coalition Government and Parliamentary Scrutiny." *American Journal of Political Science* 48 (1): 13-27.

Martin, Lanny W., and Georg Vanberg. 2005. "Coalition Policymaking and Legislative Review." *American Political Science Review* 99 (1): 93-106.

Martin, Lanny W., and Georg Vanberg. 2011. *Parliaments and Coalitions: The Role of Legislative Institutions in Multiparty Governance.* Oxford: Oxford University Press.

Mattson, Ingvar. 1995. "Private Members' Initiatives and Amendments." In *Parliaments and Majority Rule in Western Europe*, ed. Herbert Döring. Frankfurt am Main: Campus, 448-87.

Mayhew, David R. 1966. *Party Loyalty among Congressmen: The Difference between Democrats and Republicans, 1947-1962.* Cambridge: Harvard University Press.

Mayhew, David R. 1974. *Congress: The Electoral Connection.* New Haven: Yale University Press.

McCormick, Robert E., and Robert D. Tollison. 1981. *Politicians, Legislation, and the Economy: An Inquiry into the Interest Group Theory of Government.* Boston: Martin Nijhoff.

Messerschmidt, Romy. 2005. "Fraktionen in der Nationalversammlung: Von 'Problemkindern' zu verlässlichen Akteuren im französischen Regierungssystem." In *Frankreichs V. Republik: Ein Regierungssystem im Wandel*, ed. Joachim Schild and Henrik Uterwedde. Wiesbaden: VS Verlag für Sozialwissenschaften, 61-84.

Mezey, Michael L. 1994. "New Perspectives on Parliamentary Systems: A Review Article." *Legislative Studies Quarterly* 19 (3): 429-41.

Miller, Warren E., and Donald E. Stokes. 1963. "Constituency Influence in Congress." *American Political Science Review* 57 (1): 45-56.

Müller, Wolfgang C., and Kaare Strøm, eds. 1999. *Policy, Office, or Votes? How Parties in Western Europe Make Hard Decisions.* Cambridge: Cambridge University Press.

Nannestad, Peter. 2008. "Gesetzgebung im politischen System Dänemarks." In *Gesetzgebung in Westeuropa*, ed. Wolfgang Ismayr. Wiesbaden: VS Verlag für Sozialwissenschaften, 133-57.

Nason, Guy P. 2001. "Early Day Motions: Exploring Backbench Opinion during 1997-2000." Unpublished manuscript.

Nordhaus, William D. 1975. "The Political Business Cycle." *Review of Economic Studies* 42 (2): 169-90.

Norton, Philip. 1988. "The Changing Face of Parliament." *Contemporary Record* 2 (3): 2-6.

Norton, Philip, and David M. Wood. 1993. *Back from Westminster: British Members of Parliament and Their Constituents.* Lexington: University Press of Kentucky.

Olson, David M., and Philip Norton. 1996. "Legislatures in Democratic Transition." *Journal of Legislative Studies* 2 (1): 1-15.

Page, Benjamin I., Robert Y. Shapiro, Paul W. Gronke, and Robert M. Rosenberg. 1984. "Constituency, Party, and Representation in Congress." *Public Opinion Quarterly* 48 (4): 741-56.

Pelinka, Anton. 2008. "Gesetzgebung im politischen System Österreichs." In *Gesetzgebung in Westeuropa*, ed. Wolfgang Ismayr. Wiesbaden: VS Verlag für Sozialwissenschaften, 431-61.

Pesonen, Pertti. 1963. "Close and Safe State Elections in Massachusetts." *Midwest Journal of Political Science* 7 (1): 54-70.

Pétry, François, and Benoît Collette. 2009. "Measuring How Political Parties Keep Their Promises: A Positive Perspective from Political Science." In *Do They Walk Like They Talk? Speech and Action in Policy Processes*, ed. Louis M. Imbeau. Dordrecht: Springer, 65-82.

Pitkin, Hanna Fenichel. 1967. *The Concept of Representation.* Berkeley: University of California Press.

Pomper, Gerald M. 1968. *Elections in America: Control and Influence in Democratic Politics.* New York: Dodd, Mead & Company.

Powell, Bingham G. 2000. *Elections as Instruments of Democracy: Majoritarian and Proportional Visions.* New Haven: Yale University Press.

Proksch, Sven-Oliver, and Jonathan B. Slapin. 2010. "Institutional Foundations of Legislative Speech." Paper presented at the Annual Meeting of the "Arbeitskreis Handlungs- und Entscheidungstheorie" of the DVPW in Mannheim, Germany, 9-10 July 2010.

Przeworski, Adam, and Henry Teune. 1970. *The Logic of Comparative Social Inquiry.* New York: Wiley.

Rehfeld, Andrew. 2009. "Representation Rethought: On Trustees, Delegates, and Gyroscopes in the Study of Political Representation and Democracy." *American Political Science Review* 103 (2): 214-30.

Riker, William H. 1962. *The Theory of Political Coalitions.* New Haven: Yale University Press.

Rocca, Michael S., and Stacy B. Gordon. 2010. "The Position-Taking Value of Bill Sponsorship in Congress." *Political Research Quarterly* 63 (2): 387-97.

Rocca, Michael S., and Gabriel R. Sanchez. 2008. "The Effect of Race and Ethnicity on Bill Sponsorship and Cosponsorship in Congress." *American Politics Research* 36 (1): 130-52.

Rölle, Daniel. 2000. "Wahlprogramme: Richtschnur parlamentarischen Handelns." *Zeitschrift für Parlamentsfragen* 4: 820-33.

Rose, Richard. 1980. *Do Parties Make a Difference?* London: Macmillan and Chatham.

Rosenthal, Howard, and Erik Voeten. 2004. "Analyzing Roll Calls with Perfect Spatial Voting: France 1946-1958." *American Journal of Political Science* 48 (3): 620-32.

Rousseau, Jean-Jacques. 1762. "The Social Contract or Principles of Political Right." Book III, Chapter 15. Available on http://www.constitution.org/jjr/socon_03.htm, accessed on 4 August 2011.

Rubin, Donald B. 1995. "Bayes, Neyman, and Calibration." *Sociological Methodology* 25: 473-79.

Rudzio, Wolfgang. 2006. *Das politische System der Bundesrepublik Deutschland.* 7th ed. Wiesbaden: VS Verlag für Sozialwissenschaften.

Saalfeld, Thomas. 2000a. "Members of Parliament and Governments in Western Europe: Agency Relations and Problems of Oversight." *European Journal of Political Research* 37 (3): 353-76.

Saalfeld, Thomas. 2000b. "Bureaucratisation, Coordination and Competition: Parliamentary Party Groups in the German Bundestag." In *Parliamentary Party Groups in European Democracies: Political Parties behind Closed Doors*, ed. Knut Heidar and Ruud Koole. New York: Routledge, 23-38.

Saalfeld, Thomas. 2008a. "Gesetzgebung im politischen System Großbritanniens." In *Gesetzgebung in Westeuropa*, ed. Wolfgang Ismayr. Wiesbaden: VS Verlag für Sozialwissenschaften, 159-99.

Saalfeld, Thomas. 2008b. "Gesetzgebung im politischen System der Irischen Republik." In *Gesetzgebung in Westeuropa*, ed. Wolfgang Ismayr. Wiesbaden: VS Verlag für Sozialwissenschaften, 201-27.

Santaolalla, Fernando. 2008. "Gesetzgebung im politischen System Spaniens." In *Gesetzgebung in Westeuropa*, ed. Wolfgang Ismayr. Wiesbaden: VS Verlag für Sozialwissenschaften, 513-57.

Sattler, Thomas, John R. Freeman, and Patrick T. Brandt. 2008. "Political Accountability and the Room to Maneuver." *Comparative Political Studies* 41 (9): 1212-39.

Schiller, Wendy J. 1995. "Senators as Political Entrepreneurs: Using Bill Sponsorship to Shape Legislative Agendas." *American Journal of Political Science* 39 (1): 186-203.

Schmidt, Manfred G. 1996. "When Parties Matter: A Review of the Possibilities and Limits of Partisan Influence on Public Policy." *European Journal of Political Research* 30 (3): 155-83.

Schneider, Gerald, and Gabriele Ruoff. 2010. "Quantitative Methoden." In *Handbuch der Internationalen Politik*, ed. Carlo Masala, Frank Sauer, and Andreas Wilhelm. Wiesbaden: VS Verlag für Sozialwissenschaften, 232-40.

Schroen, Michael. 2008. "Gesetzgebung im politischen System Luxemburgs." In *Gesetzgebung in Westeuropa*, ed. Wolfgang Ismayr. Wiesbaden: VS Verlag für Sozialwissenschaften, 349-81.

Schwindt-Bayer, Leslie A., and Renato Corbetta. 2004. "Gender Turnover and Roll-Call Voting in the U.S. House of Representatives." *Legislative Studies Quarterly* 29 (2): 215-29.

Sebaldt, Martin. 1992. *Die Thematisierungsfunktion der Opposition: Die parlamentarische Minderheit des Deutschen Bundestags als innovative Kraft im politischen System der Bundesrepublik Deutschland.* Frankfurt am Main: Lang.

Shepsle, Kenneth A., and Barry R. Weingast. 1981. "Structure-Induced Equilibrium and Legislative Choice." *Public Choice* 37 (3): 503-19.

Sieberer, Ulrich. 2006. "Party Unity in Parliamentary Democracies: A Comparative Analysis." *Journal of Legislative Studies* 12 (2): 150-78.
Sieberer, Ulrich. 2010. "Behavioral Consequences of Mixed Electoral Systems: Deviating Voting Behavior of District and List MPs in the German Bundestag." *Electoral Studies* 29 (3): 484-96.
Stratmann, Thomas. 2000. "Congressional Voting Over Legislative Careers: Shifting Positions and Changing Constraints." *American Political Science Review* 94 (3): 665-76.
Stratmann, Thomas, and Martin Baur. 2002. "Plurality Rule, Proportional Representation, and the German Bundestag: How Incentives to Pork-Barrel Differ across Electoral Systems." *American Journal of Political Science* 46 (3): 506-14.
Strøm, Kaare. 1990. *Minority Government and Majority Rule.* Cambridge: Cambridge University Press.
Sulkin, Tracy. 2005. *Issue Politics in Congress.* Cambridge: Cambridge University Press.
Thiébault, Jean-Louis, and Bernard Dolez. 2000. "Parliamentary Parties in the French Fifth Republic." In *Parliamentary Party Groups in European Democracies: Political Parties behind Closed Doors*, ed. Knut Heidar and Ruud Koole. London: Routledge, 57-70.
Thies, Michael F. 2001. "Keeping Tabs on Partners: The Logic of Delegation in Coalition Governments." *American Journal of Political Science* 45 (3): 580-98.
Timmermans, Arco, Peter Scholten, and Steven Oostlander. 2008. "Gesetzgebung im politischen System der Niederlande." In *Gesetzgebung in Westeuropa*, ed. Wolfgang Ismayr. Wiesbaden: VS Verlag für Sozialwissenschaften, 271-301.
Toshkov, Dimiter. 2011. "Public Opinion and Policy Output in the European Union: A Lost Relationship." *European Union Politics* 12 (2): 169-91.
Trantas, Georgios. 1995. "Comparing Legislative Instruments across Nations." In *Parliaments and Majority Rule in Western Europe*, ed. Herbert Döring. Frankfurt am Main: Campus, 615-27.
Tsebelis, George. 1995. "Veto Players and Law Production in Parliamentary Democracies." In *Parliaments and Majority Rule in Western Europe*, ed. Herbert Döring. Frankfurt am Main: Campus, 83-111.
Tsebelis, George. 2002. *Veto Players: How Political Institutions Work.* Princeton: Princeton University Press.
Tsebelis, George, and Jeanette Money. 1997. *Bicameralism.* Cambridge: Cambridge University Press.
Van Schoor, Willy. 1972. *Wetsvoorstellen als middel tot parlementair wetgevend initiatief in Belgie.* M.A. Thesis. Leuven: Katholieke Universiteit te Leuven.
Victor, Jennifer Nicoll. 2011. "Legislating Versus Campaigning: The Legislative Behavior of Higher Office-Seekers." *American Politics Research* 39 (1): 3-31.
Vliegenthart, Rens, Stefaan Walgrave, and Corine Meppelink. 2011. "Inter-Party Agenda-Setting in the Belgian Parliament: The Role of Party Characteristics and Competition." *Political Studies* 59 (2): 368-88.
Weber, Peter. 2008. "Gesetzgebung im politischen System Italiens." In *Gesetzgebung in Westeuropa*, ed. Wolfgang Ismayr. Wiesbaden: VS Verlag für Sozialwissenschaften, 463-511.

Welch, Susan. 1985. "Are Women More Liberal than Men in the U.S. Congress?" *Legislative Studies Quarterly* 10 (1): 125-34.

Wessels, Bernhard. 2004. "Abgeordnetenbefragung 2003: Kurzfassung und Dokumentation der Ergebnisse." Available on http://www.wzb.eu/de/zkd/dsl/pdf/Ber-fin1-all1.pdf, accessed on 4 June 2011.

Whitby, Kenny J. 2002. "Bill Sponsorship and Intraracial Voting among African American Representatives." *American Politics Research* 30 (1): 93-109.

Wiberg, Matti. 1995. "Parliamentary Questioning: Control by Communication?" In *Parliaments and Majority Rule in Western Europe*, ed. Herbert Döring. Frankfurt am Main: Campus, 179-222.

Wiberg, Matti. 2004. *Lainsäädäntötuotos Suomessa Valtiopäivillä 1945-2002: Peruskartoitus*. Turku: Turun Yliopisto.

Wilson, Walter Clark. 2010. "Descriptive Representation and Latino Interest Bill Sponsorship in Congress." *Social Science Quarterly* 91 (4): 1043-62.

Woon, Jonathan. 2008. "Bill Sponsorship in Congress: The Moderating Effect of Agenda Positions on Legislative Proposals." *Journal of Politics* 70 (1): 201-16.

Woydt, Malte. 2008. "Gesetzgebung im politischen System Belgiens." In *Gesetzgebung in Westeuropa*, ed. Wolfgang Ismayr. Wiesbaden: VS Verlag für Sozialwissenschaften, 303-47.

Woyke, Wichard. 1999. "Das politische System Belgiens." In *Die politischen Systeme Westeuropas*, ed. Wolfgang Ismayr. 2nd ed. Opladen: Leske+Budrich, 365-88.

Zervakis, Peter A., and Antonis Chanos. 2008. "Gesetzgebung im politischen System Griechenlands." In *Gesetzgebung in Westeuropa*, ed. Wolfgang Ismayr. Wiesbaden: VS Verlag für Sozialwissenschaften, 615-51.

MIX
Papier aus verantwortungsvollen Quellen
Paper from responsible sources
FSC® C105338
FSC
www.fsc.org

If you have any concerns about our products,
you can contact us on
ProductSafety@springernature.com

In case Publisher is established outside the EU,
the EU authorized representative is:
Springer Nature Customer Service Center GmbH
Europaplatz 3, 69115 Heidelberg, Germany

Printed by Libri Plureos GmbH
in Hamburg, Germany